Transformation
of the God-Image

Marie-Louise von Franz, Honorary Patron

**Studies in Jungian Psychology
by Jungian Analysts**

Daryl Sharp, General Editor

Transformation of the God-Image

An Elucidation of Jung's *Answer to Job*

Edward F. Edinger

Edited with a Foreword by
Lawrence W. Jaffe

Thanks to Nancy Berry for her diligent work on the typescript, to
Susan Murphy for her advice and encouragement, and to Isabel
Mavity for her generous support of the project.—Lawrence W. Jaffe.

Canadian Cataloguing in Publication Data

Edinger, Edward F. (Edward Ferdinand), 1922-
  Transformation of the God-image

(Studies in Jungian psychology by Jungian analysts; 54)

Includes bibliographical references and index.

ISBN 0-919123-55-4

1. Jung, C.G. (Carl Gustav), 1875-1961. Antwort auf Hiob.
2. Bible. O.T. Job—Criticism, interpretation, etc.
3. Image of God. 4. Religion—Philosophy.
I. Title. II. Series.

BL51.E35 1992   223'.106   C92-093051-4

INNER CITY BOOKS
Box 1271, Station Q, Toronto, Canada M4T 2P4
Telephone (416) 927-0355
FAX 416-924-1814

Honorary Patron: Marie-Louise von Franz.
Publisher and General Editor: Daryl Sharp.
Senior Editor: Victoria Cowan.

INNER CITY BOOKS was founded in 1980 to promote the
understanding and practical application of the work of C.G. Jung.

Cover: Painting of a dream image, by C.G. Jung, 1920.
[From Aniela Jaffé, ed., *C.G. Jung: Word and Image* (Bollingen
Series XCVII:2); Princeton: Princeton University Press, 1979]

Frontispiece: Photo by Margareta Fellerer, Ascona.

Printed and bound in Canada by
John Deyell Company Limited.

Contents

Foreword 7

1   Introduction 11

2   Prefatory Note, Paragraphs 553-559 and the Book of Job 21

3   Paragraphs 560-576 32

4   Paragraphs 577-608 42

5   Paragraphs 609-624 53

6   Paragraphs 625-648 63

7   Paragraphs 649-661 73

8   Paragraphs 662-687 and the Book of Enoch 82

9   Paragraphs 688-712 92

10 Paragraphs 713-733 102

11 Paragraphs 734-747 113

12 Paragraphs 748-758, Assumption of Mary and Summary 124

Bibliography 136

Index 138

See final page for other titles by Inner City Books

Foreword

Despite the Biblical imagery, this book is not concerned with traditional religion. Its subject, rather, is psychology, the scientific study of the soul. References are to Job, God and Christ because our deepest feelings still resonate to that imagery. Put another way, the reason for the Biblical references is because "Jungian psychology has the task of introducing to the world a new world view."[1] The roots of this new world view lie in the Judeo-Christian myth.

If, as Edinger predicts, Jung's works are one day read as Scripture once was—for sustenance of our souls, for moving words that touch us to the heart, for reassurance, guidance and orientation—*Answer to Job* will surely occupy a unique place in the Jungian canon. The special status of *Answer to Job* as the most complete statement of Jung's essential message has long been acknowledged by Jungians who have discussed it in countless seminars and conferences since its publication in 1952.

What has sparked all this interest is that the central theme of *Answer to Job*—the transformation of God through human consciousness—is the central theme, too, of Jungian psychology. Not long before his death Jung himself affirmed its importance, remarking that "he would like to rewrite all of his books except *Answer to Job,* but he would leave that one just as it stands."[2]

Now comes a definitive study of *Answer to Job* by Edinger, in his usual trenchant style, at once erudite and down-to-earth, thoughtful and heartfelt.

For a generation Edinger has been in the forefront of those who have carried forward the work of the great Swiss psychiatrist Carl Gustav Jung. Edinger is a founding member of both the C.G. Jung Foundation for Analytical Psychology of New York and the Jung Institute of New York. He served as president of the Institute from 1968 through 1979, and was also a member of its faculty. His ten

---

[1] Edward F. Edinger, *Aion,* lecture series available on audiotape from the C.G. Jung Institute of Los Angeles.

[2] Marie-Louise von Franz, *C.G. Jung: His Myth in Our Time,* p. 161.

7

books and more than fifty published articles reveal four major areas of interest: clinical, cultural, alchemical and the psychological redemption of traditional religion.[3] A single unifying theme runs through them all, namely the ego's encounter with and relation to the Self, Jung's term for the regulating center of the psyche.

At a recent Jungian conference on the inner child where the work of developmental psychologists was emphasized, a participant rose in the final moments to ask how we psychotherapists could bear to listen hour after hour, day after day, to the stories of terrible psychic wounds inflicted on children, who upon becoming parents unconsciously repeat the pattern.

I replied somewhat as follows: "This is where Jung comes in. He says that the enlightened human consciousness breaks the chain of suffering and thereby acquires a metaphysical and cosmic significance. We therapists sometimes see this process operating in our daily work. Without the intervention of consciousness the chain repeats itself."[4]

Several people thanked me for reminding them of Jung's words, which in fact I had in mind only because I had recently heard them reformulated by Edinger.[5]

Answer to Job contains the kernel, the essence, of the Jungian myth, and Edinger's study of it evokes that essence with unequaled clarity and power. This is not to say that everything in it will be crystal clear at first glance, but it is possible that the receptive reader will catch a whisper of Jung's meaning in some word or phrase, and this will repay the effort manyfold.

Apart from minor stylistic revisions, the following is a transcript of the course of twelve lectures given by Edinger at the C.G. Jung Institute of Los Angeles in the fall of 1989.

Lawrence W. Jaffe
Jungian analyst, Berkeley

---

[3] See bibliography for a complete list of Edinger's published books.

[4] See Jung, *Letters,* vol. 2, p. 311.

[5] *An American Jungian: Edward F. Edinger in Conversation with Lawrence Jaffe* (videotape). See also below, p. 61.

Whoever knows God has an effect on him.
—C.G. Jung, *Answer to Job.*

Jung at the age of 75

1
Introduction

Generally speaking, *Answer to Job* can be considered a depth-psychological examination of the Judeo-Christian myth, which is at the core of the Western psyche. Another way of putting it is that *Answer to Job* is a continuation of *Aion.*[6] Jung says as much himself:

> The most immediate cause of my writing the book is perhaps to be found in certain problems discussed in my book *Aion,* especially the problems of Christ as a symbolic figure and of the antagonism Christ-Antichrist represented in the traditional zodiacal symbolism of the two fishes.[7]

The basic issue in *Aion* is the double or bipolar nature of the Christian God-image which unfolded itself in the course of the history of the Christian aeon. Beginning with the image of the son of Yahweh, Christ, in the first half of the aeon, a gradual *enantiodromia*[8] took place and the opposite side—the *bad* son, the Antichrist pole—of the bipolar deity began to manifest in the second half of the Christian aeon. *Answer to Job* continues the study of the Western God-image, and in particular explores how human consciousness changes the nature of that God-image.

In order to avoid confusion as you are reading *Answer to Job* it's important to distinguish three different aspects, or versions, of the Western God-image:

1) The God-image as pictured in the Old Testament—Yahweh.

2) The God-image as pictured in Christian theology. This corresponds to the image that Christ delineated—the God of Love.

3) The God-image as experienced psychologically by modern men and women.

---

[6] CW 9ii. (CW refers throughout to *The Collected Works of C.G. Jung)*

[7] "Prefatory Note," *Psychology and Religion,* CW 11, p. 357.

[8] Running counter to. "I use the term enantiodromia for the emergence of the unconscious opposite in the course of time." ("Definitions," *Psychological Types,* CW 6, par. 709)

These are, in short, the Old Testament God, the New Testament God and God as experienced psychologically.

Jung refers to all three of these intermittently and interweaves them. That's why I want to make crystal clear that one is really dealing with three different entities, because otherwise you can get lost and confused as to what Jung is getting at.

1) *The God-image as pictured in the Old Testament.* This is the God-image that was experienced by Job. It is characterized by a combination of opposites: Yahweh is both kind and wrathful, just and unjust, and he contains these opposites without contradiction because no consciousness has ever intervened to challenge the contradiction. Job, in his encounter with Yahweh, becomes that consciousness, perceives the contradiction and thereby generates the challenge to Yahweh.

2) *The God-image as pictured in Christian theology.* In Christian theology the God-image of Yahweh has undergone a transformation by the Incarnation. It's never said so outright, it would be kind of scandalous to say it outright. But in the legendary and marginal material it's stated quite explicitly that Yahweh was tamed in the lap of the Virgin. He underwent a transformation, that's the idea, by being incarnated as man. The Yahweh God-image is born as a man, and in the process of that incarnation he takes on a one-sided goodness. He becomes exclusively the loving, benevolent God who has no darkness in him. That is represented by the figure of Christ who is theologically considered to be the son of God. But as Jung points out, he's only one of two sons. In the background is the other son, Satan, the Antichrist, who is going to have his day sooner or later.

3) *The God-image as experienced psychologically* by modern men and women takes us up to the present time—to our own individual experience which we need to bring to this study of *Answer to Job* in order to make it really relevant psychologically. Jung has had a lot to say about how the God-image is experienced psychologically and I want to spend most of the remainder of our time today giving examples of Jung's experience of the God-image.

Here's how he put it in his *Visions Seminars:*

For the collective unconscious we could use the word God. . . .

You all know what the collective unconscious is, you have certain dreams that carry the hallmark of the collective unconscious: instead of dreaming of Aunt This or Uncle That, you dream of a lion, and then the analyst will tell you that that is a mythological motif, and you will understand that it is the collective unconscious. So you get the collective unconscious right there. This God is no longer miles of abstract space away from you in an extra-mundane sphere. This divinity is not a concept in a theological textbook, or in the Bible; it is an immediate thing, it happens in your dreams at night, it causes you to have pains in the stomach, diarrhea, constipation, a whole host of neuroses. . . . If you try to formulate it, to think what the collective unconscious is after all, you wind up by concluding that it is what the Prophets were concerned with; it sounds exactly like some things in the Old Testament. There God sends plagues upon people, he burns their bones in the night, he injures their kidneys, he causes all sorts of troubles. Then you come naturally to the dilemma: Is that really God? Is God a neurosis? . . . Now that is a shocking dilemma, I admit, but when you think consistently and logically, you come to the conclusion that God *is* a most shocking problem. And that is the truth, God has shocked people out of their wits. Think what he did to poor old Hosea. He was a respectable man and he had to marry a prostitute. Probably he suffered from a strange kind of mother complex.[9]

That one passage will give you an idea of what the God-image is when encountered psychologically. I'm going to give you further examples. In the 1937 Terry lectures, Jung discusses a patient who had a cancer phobia. He was convinced he had cancer, and no amount of medical examination could convince him otherwise.

What, then, shall we say to our patient with the imaginary cancer? I would tell him: "Yes, my friend, you are really suffering from a cancer-like thing, you really do harbour in yourself a deadly evil. However, it will not kill your body, because it is imaginary. But it will eventually kill your soul. It has already spoilt and even poisoned your human relations and your personal happiness and it will go on growing until it has swallowed your whole psychic existence. So that in the end you will not be a human being any more, but an evil destructive tumour."[10]

---

9 Vol. 2, p. 391.
10 "Psychology and Religion," *Psychology and Religion,* CW 11, par. 19.

Jung continues:

It is, to my mind, a fatal mistake to regard the human psyche as a purely personal affair. . . . [If] some slight trouble occurs, perhaps in the form of an unforeseen and somewhat unusual event, instantly instinctual forces are called up, forces which appear to be wholly unexpected, new, and strange. They can no longer be explained in terms of personal motives, being comparable rather to certain primitive occurrences like panics at solar eclipses and the like. . . .

The change of character brought about by the uprush of collective forces is amazing. A gentle and reasonable being can be transformed into a maniac or a savage beast. . . . As a matter of fact, we are constantly living on the edge of a volcano, and there is, so far as we know, no way of protecting ourselves from a possible outburst . . . .

. . . It only needs a neurosis to conjure up a force that cannot be dealt with by rational means. Our cancer case shows clearly how impotent man's reason and intellect are against the most palpable nonsense. I always advise my patients to take such obvious but invincible nonsense as the manifestation of a power and a meaning they have not yet understood. . . . Our patient is confronted with a power of will and suggestion more than equal to anything his consciousness can put against it. In this precarious situation it would be bad strategy to convince him that in some incomprehensible way he is at the back of his own symptom, secretly inventing and supporting it. Such a suggestion would instantly paralyse his fighting spirit, and he would get demoralized. It is far better for him to understand that his complex is an autonomous power [i.e., God] directed against his conscious personality.[11]

This man was caught by his phobia. That's how the God-image manifested in him.

In an interview he gave not long before his death, Jung described his experience of the God-image in these words:

To this day God is the name by which I designate all things which cross my willful path, violently and recklessly, all things which upset my subjective views, plans and intentions and change the course of my life for better or worse.[12]

---

11 Ibid., pars. 24-26.
12 Interview published in *Good Housekeeping Magazine,* December 1961. See also *Letters,* vol. 2, p. 525.

In a letter to Erich Neumann concerning *Answer to Job* Jung refers to his experience of God in this way:

> I could no longer consider the average reader. Rather he has to consider *me*. [This is why it is so hard for us to understand *Answer to Job,* you see—because this is the attitude he's writing it out of.] I had to pay this tribute to the pitiless fact of my old age. With the undimmed prospect of all-around incomprehension I could exercise no suasions and no *captatio benevolentiae* [currying favor]; there was no hope of funnelling knowledge into fools. Not in my livery, but "naked and bare I must go down to the grave," fully aware of the outrage my nakedness will provoke. But what is that compared with the arrogance I had to summon up in order to be able to insult God? . . .
>
> The book is about the Canonical God-image. This is our prime concern, and not a general philosophical concept of God. God is always specific and always locally valid, otherwise he would be ineffectual. The Western God-image is the valid one for me, whether I assent to it intellectually or not. I do not go in for religious philosophy, but am held in thrall, almost crushed, and defend myself as best I can. . . . This is local, barbaric, infantile, and abysmally unscientific.[13]

That's the quality of the God-image and the God-experience that Jung had and out of which *Answer to Job* was written.

In another letter written a few days earlier, he's replying to an inquiry about *Answer to Job* in which the correspondent had commented on Jung's sarcasm.

> What offends you bothered me too. I would have liked to avoid sarcasm and mockery but couldn't, for that is the way I felt and if I had not said so it would have been all the worse, but hidden. I realized only afterwards that they have their place as expressing resistance to God's nature, which sets us at odds with ourselves. I had to wrench myself free of God, so to speak, in order to find that unity in myself which God seeks through man. . . .
>
> Sarcasm is certainly not a pretty quality, but I am forced to use even means I find reprehensible in order to deliver myself from the Father. God himself uses very different means to jolt these human beings of his into consciousness. It has not yet been forgotten, I

---

[13] *Letters,* vol. 2, p. 32.

hope, what happened in Germany and what is happening day after day in Russia. Job's suffering never ceases and multiplies a million-fold. I cannot avert my eyes from that. By remaining with the Father, I deny him the human being in whom he could unify himself and become One, and how can I help him better than by becoming One myself? . . .

Sarcasm is the means by which we hide our hurt feelings from ourselves, and from this you can see how very much the knowledge of God has wounded me, and how very much I would have preferred to remain a child in the Father's protection and shun the problem of opposites. It is probably even more difficult to deliver oneself from good than from evil. But without sin there is no breaking away from the good Father; sarcasm plays the corresponding role in this case.[14]

In a letter to Morton Kelsey, Jung continues to speak of his experience of God:

[In] discussing the admittedly anthropomorphic image of Yahweh . . . I do not apply metaphysical judgements. From this methodological standpoint I gain the necessary freedom of criticism. The absence of human morality in Yahweh is a stumbling block which cannot be overlooked, as little as the fact that Nature, i.e., God's creation, does not give us enough reason to believe it to be purposive or reasonable in the human sense. We miss reason and moral values. . . . It is therefore obvious that the Yahwistic image or conception of the deity is less than [that of] certain human specimens: the image of a personified brutal force and of an unethical and non-spiritual mind, yet inconsistent enough to exhibit traits of kindness and generosity besides a violent power-drive. It is the picture of a sort of nature-demon and at the same time of a primitive chieftain aggrandized to a colossal size. . . .

This image owes its existence [to certain experiences of the prophets]. . . .

This most shocking defectuosity of the God-image ought to be explained or understood. The nearest analogy to it is our experience of the unconscious: it is a psyche whose nature can only be described by paradoxes: it is personal as well as impersonal, moral and amoral, just and unjust, ethical and unethical, of cunning intelligence and at the same time blind, immensely strong and extremely weak, etc.

---

14 Ibid., p. 28.

This is the psychic foundation which produces the raw material for our conceptual structures. The unconscious is a piece of Nature our mind cannot comprehend. It can only sketch models.[15]

Jung's letters give us a picture of how he came to write *Answer to Job* in the spring of 1951. It wasn't the result of a rational decision. He was seventy-five years old and in the midst of a febrile illness. It was virtually dictated to him from the unconscious and as soon as it was completed, his illness was over.

In a letter to Aniela Jaffé on July 18, 1951, Jung wrote:

If there is anything like the spirit seizing one by the scruff of the neck, it was the way this book came into being.[16]

And a couple of years later:

The book "came to me" during the fever of an illness. It was as if accompanied by the great music of a Bach or a Handel. . . . I just had the feeling of listening to a great composition, or rather of being at a concert.[17]

And again:

My criticism of the Yahwistic God-image is for you what the experience was for me: a drama that was not mine to control. I felt myself utterly the *causa ministerialis* of my book. It came upon me suddenly and unexpectedly during a feverish illness. I feel its content as an unfolding of the divine consciousness in which I participate, like it or not.[18]

Also Esther Harding told me that during his illness a figure sat on his bedpost and dictated *Answer to Job* to him. He says something about this in one of his letters, too. He's responding to a review of *Answer to Job:*

Allow me to tell you that I am profoundly grateful to you for your most remarkably objective review of my uncouth attempt to disturb the obnoxious somnolence of the guardians. That is the way in

---

15 Ibid., p. 434.
16 Ibid., p. 20.
17 Ibid., p. 116.
18 Ibid., p. 112.

which this damnable little book looks to me. . . . I would not have written this thing. I had kept away from it studiously. I had published before the volume *Aion* in polite language and as much man-made as possible. It was not sufficient apparently, because I got ill and when I was in the fever it caught me and brought me down to writing despite my fever, my age, and my heart that is none too good. I can assure you I am a moral coward as long as possible. As a good little bourgeois citizen, I am lying low and concealed as deeply as possible, still shocked by the amount of the indiscretions I have committed, swearing to myself that there would be no more of it because I want peace and friendly neighbourhood and a good conscience and the sleep of the just. Why should I be the unspeakable fool to jump into the cauldron?

Well, I don't want to be melodramatic. This is just for your personal information. I have no merit and no proper guilt since I got to it "like a dog to a kick," as we say. And the little moral coward I am goes on whining: Why should I be always the one that collects all available kicks?

I tell you these things because you have been nice, just, and lenient with me. The attribute "coarse" is mild in comparison to what you feel when God dislocates your hip or when he slays the first-born. . . .

That is *one side* of my experiences with what is called "God." "Coarse" is too weak a word for it. "Crude," "violent," "cruel," "bloody," "hellish," "demonic" would be better. That I was not downright blasphemous I owe to my domestication and polite cowardice. And at each step I felt hindered by a beatific vision of which I'd better say nothing.[19]

But he did say something about it in *Memories, Dreams, Reflections.*[20] In other words he also experienced the opposite of the dark side of God.

I think another self-description of Jung and his experience of writing *Answer to Job* is implicit in his description of John, the author of the Book of Revelation:

---

[19] Ibid., pp. 155f.

[20] See p. 294, where Jung describes his *coniunctio* visions during his near-fatal illness in 1944. This passage is also quoted in Edinger, *The Bible and the Psyche: Individuation Symbolism in the Old Testament,* pp. 144-145.

In *confinio mortis* [the edge of death] and in the evening of a long and eventful life a man will often see immense vistas of time stretching out before him. Such a man no longer lives in the everyday world and in the vicissitudes of personal relationships, but in the sight of many aeons and in the movement of ideas as they pass from century to century.[21]

That description fits Jung, I think, and it's out of that state of mind that *Answer to Job* was written.

*

Whenever I start to consider a work the first thing I look at is the title. I assume that titles will have depths of meaning that bear some reflection—that they're not just casual labels. This book is titled *Answer to Job*. Jung tells us in the course of the work what the first level of meaning of that title is: Since Yahweh treated Job unjustly, and since that fact was registered consciously by Job, the crime that Yahweh committed against Job on account of his unconsciousness, required rectification, required an answer. And Jung tells us, in the book, that Yahweh's answer to his unjust treatment of Job was his incarnation as man. Since in his encounter with Yahweh, Job, as the image of humanity, had displayed a consciousness superior to Yahweh's, Yahweh was obliged to catch up with him morally, so to speak, and the answer was for Yahweh to become man. That's the obvious first-level of meaning of the title, *Answer to Job*.

I think there's a second level of meaning, too. And I suspect that Jung was aware of it, as well. The second level of meaning is that *Jung* is providing the answer to Job. Although the first level of meaning was provided two thousand years ago, nobody has realized that that was the answer to Job. If something doesn't reach consciousness, it doesn't exist. Jung's insight about this state of affairs effectively answers Job and of course not only the Job of antiquity but Job as the archetype of *all* of suffering humanity that has been obliged to suffer unjustly because of the nature of reality. Because, as Jung tells us here, "God is Reality itself." (par. 631)

---

[21] "Answer to Job," *Psychology and Religion,* CW 11, par. 717. [Subsequent references are to paragraph number only, and in the main text, except for the Prefatory Note, where the paragraphs are not numbered.—Ed.]

Finally, just one further remark concerning the magnitude of this work. Marie-Louise von Franz, in her biography of Jung, tells us that this is the one work with which Jung was completely satisfied.[22] He would like to have had the opportunity to rewrite all of his other works but with regard to *Answer to Job* he was content to leave it just as it stands.

We may not be able to appreciate the full meaning of Jung's *Answer to Job* in our brief study. In my opinion it will take centuries for the meaning of this work to be assimilated. But a good attitude with which to approach it is one in which you keep in mind its magnitude and when you run across something you don't understand, don't assume it's a failure on Jung's part.

---

[22] See above, note 2.

2
Prefatory Note, Paragraphs 553-559
and The Book of Job

Last time we ended with a discussion of the two levels of meaning of
the title of *Answer to Job.* Today we will continue in sequence with a
discussion of the Prefatory Note and the next chapter, *Lectori Benevolo,* and we will conclude with another look at the Book of Job of
the Old Testament which I asked you to reread.

Prefatory Note

In his Prefatory Note Jung tells us that the occasion for writing
Answer to Job (to put it in a nutshell) was his encounter with the
problem of the opposites. And he tells us that this problem presented
itself to him in two different areas:

1) The problem of the opposites in the Christian God-image which
he had been working on in *Aion.*

2) The opposites as encountered in alchemy.

Let me read again Jung's words:

> The most immediate cause of my writing the book is perhaps to be
> found in certain problems discussed in my book *Aion,* especially the
> problems of Christ as a symbolic figure and of the antagonism
> Christ-Antichrist, represented in the traditional zodiacal symbolism
> of the two fishes.[23]

He then goes on to criticize the idea of the *privatio boni,* writing:

> Psychological experience shows that whatever we call "good" is bal-
> anced by an equally substantial "bad" or "evil."[24]

So the opposites Jung engaged are those of good and evil.

As a kind of corollary to his encounter with the opposites in the
Christian God-image, Jung addresses the question, "Whence evil?"

---

[23] *Psychology and Religion,* CW 11, p. 357.
[24] Ibid.

He says:

> Later Christianity . . . is dualistic, inasmuch as it splits off one half
> of the opposites, personified in Satan, [who] is *eternal* in his state of
> damnation. This crucial question [of "whence evil"] . . . forms the
> point of departure for the Christian theory of Redemption.[25]

What Jung means by that is that the Christian theory of redemption posits the source of evil to reside in man. Man is the source of
evil and therefore man is in need of redemption. That's the point of
departure for the Christian theory of redemption. Practically speaking
it locates evil in man but then theologically speaking it locates evil in
the hypostasized figure of Satan. So that you've got a double message there, an ambiguity that has never been faced squarely until
Jung faced it in this book.

So that's the encounter with the opposites in the Christian God-
image. And Jung says the other place where he encounters the opposites is in alchemy:

> The study of medieval natural philosophy [that's alchemy]—of the
> greatest importance to psychology—made me try to find an answer
> to the question: what image of God did these old philosophers have?
> Or rather: how should the symbols which supplement their image of
> God be understood? All this pointed to a *complexio oppositorum* and
> thus recalled again the story of Job to my mind: Job who expected
> help from God against God. This most peculiar fact presupposes a
> similar conception of the opposites in God.[26]

You see his basic concern is dealing with the psychological problem of the opposites. And I'll remind you that at the same time as he
wrote *Answer to Job* he was putting *Mysterium Coniunctionis* together. That wasn't published till 1955 but he worked on it over a
ten-year period. Therefore (as he actually says in *Mysterium Coniunctionis*), *Answer to Job* is a kind of appendage to that work as
well as being a kind of sequel to *Aion*. It is part of the same fabric as
both those works.

I want to call attention to a remark Jung makes about the style of

---

25 Ibid., p. 358.
26 Ibid.

writing he employs in *Answer to Job:*

> I was gripped by the urgency and difficulty of the problem and was unable to throw it off. Therefore I found myself obliged to deal with the whole problem, and I did so in the form of describing a personal experience, carried by subjective emotions. I deliberately chose this form because I wanted to avoid the impression that I had any idea of announcing an "eternal truth."[27]

I understand that remark to mean he very carefully and explicitly wrote this material out of his human wholeness. This kind of material is really very dangerous to talk about, because it's so easy to fall into an inflation. It is an example of Jung's canniness in dealing with the unconscious that he comes to this material out of human wholeness and thus avoids the inflation which would otherwise be constellated whenever one starts touching this highly numinous material. He writes this book throughout with absolute humanness. He doesn't write abstractly at all, and the earthy colloquial speech is part of his protection against inflation because it's very dangerous to talk about this level of material.

Lectori Benevolo [To the Kind Reader]

With this phrase Jung is asking for the indulgence of the reader whom he knows he's about to offend. He's approaching us with elaborate courtesy because he knows he's going to stir up rhinoceros-like affects and as he tells us in another place, rhinoceroses don't like to be surprised so they should be treated with elaborate courtesy.

That's how I understand that particular phrase, "To the Kind Reader." He's asking for our kindness in view of the offense he's about to offer. Because as soon as you begin to look honestly into the material in this book you realize that it's going to offend almost everybody. And if you're not offended, you probably don't understand what he's saying.

Either one will be offended that Jung contradicts the familiar God-image that one cherishes in one's own religious confession or formulation, either that, or if one is a secular rationalist he will be offended

---

[27] Ibid.

that Jung takes so seriously the primitive anthropomorphic God-image that rationalists have long since discredited. One or the other standpoint is going to be offended and it's quite possible that a single person will be offended at both levels at the same time. So I urge all of you to admit it—you're annoyed.

I know when I first read *Answer to Job* when it came out in translation in the fifties, what offended me was how seriously he took this Old Testament God-image, expecting something from Him. In other words I had the rationalist position. I thought, "Grow up Jung, don't you realize you mustn't expect justice? The world isn't like that." In other words I had a cynical, stoic, rationalistic attitude toward the world. That's how *I* originally experienced my offense. And I think each of you should ask yourself how you are offended, because if you locate how you are offended it will tell you something about the nature of your own unconscious assumptions and that can be a valuable bit of self-knowledge.

Next comes the motto. In the German original of *Answer to Job* this motto appears in the Latin of the Vulgate—*Doleo super te frater mi* . . . The meaning of these words is not accurately conveyed by the Authorized Version passage that appears in the English translation. The actual translation should read, "I grieve for you my brother," because he's grieving over a brother's death. This isn't just a matter of being distressed—the word *doleo* means I grieve, I suffer a loss.

The background of this quotation is highly significant. It is an utterance of David's concerning his dear friend Jonathan. Jonathan, the son of King Saul, had just died in a battle with the Philistines, along with his father. They had both perished in that same battle. And David is singing an elegy to them in which these lines appear, "O Jonathan, in your death I am stricken, I grieve for you Jonathan, my brother."[28]

Now you have to remember that this motto is directed at the "kind reader," namely at us—we who are reading it. And Jung is saying "I grieve for you my brother who is about to read this work."

Let's spend a few moments examining the Biblical context of

---

[28] 2 Sam. 1:26, Jerusalem Bible (modified).

these words: Saul was the *first* king of Israel, and although the spirit of Yahweh was with him at the outset, it turned negative and destroyed him. David was the *second* king of Israel and the spirit of Yahweh which had abandoned Saul entered David who then had a successful reign.

Now Jonathan was the son of Saul but he was a loyal friend of David, though David was destined to replace him as the king's successor. Remember that Jonathan was his beloved, loyal friend. You see, this was a moment of momentous transition between the reign of King Saul and that of King David.

In an earlier series of lectures I spoke of Saul as representing the first-stage ego and David as representing the second-stage ego.[29] The second-stage ego is the one with the right relationship to the Self. And Jonathan, the son of Saul, is caught between conflicting loyalties. Loyalty as his father's son on one hand and to the King-to-be, David, on the other hand. But he was not able to choose wholeheartedly for David. If he had he would have gone over to David's party and he would not have been with his father during the battle with the Philistines and died with him. So his residual dependence on the outworn state of being is what killed him.

I'm going into all of this because it is relevant to the way Jung perceives those who are about to read his book. It corresponds to Jung's feeling about the contemporary world to whom he is sending this book. You see, like David, he was all alone. About seven months before he died he unburdened himself in a letter to a person who had sent him a book, someone he didn't know. Here are some of the things he had to say:

> I had to understand that I was unable to make the people see what I am after. I am practically alone. There are a few who understand this and that but almost nobody sees the whole. . . . I have failed in my foremost task, to open people's eyes to the fact that man has a soul, and there is a buried treasure in the field and that our religion and philosophy is in a lamentable state.[30]

Answer to Job is written out of that kind of lonely awareness.

---

[29] See *The Bible and the Psyche,* pp. 81-82.
[30] Quoted by Gerhard Adler in "Aspects of Jung's Personality," p. 14.

Jung is aware that the readers of his book are, at best, in the same situation as Jonathan, namely caught in the old attitude and in the moment of crucial transition unable to free themselves completely to go over to the new attitude. We, like Jonathan, must perish because we are operating out of the old attitude, the standpoint of King Saul.

Now let us turn to the substance of the *Lectori Benevolo*. It's really a quite wonderful exposition of the reality of the psyche. This, you know, is probably *the* basic theme of Jungian psychology—the reality of the psyche. And Jung starts right out by telling us that he's in danger of being torn to pieces by the two parties who are in mortal conflict over psychological matters. Either the psychological imagery is embedded in a metaphysical religious context and must be taken as concretely true or the imagery can be subjected to rationalistic/reductive criticism and interpreted away—into nothing. That's what I call, elsewhere, the concretistic and the reductive fallacies. Jung says that if you're going to talk about these matters you're going to be torn apart by the two parties who take these opposing positions. Whereas what he's offering is a third position, which is that these are *psychic* truths.

There are two or three pages here that are worth many readings because the reality of the psyche is communicated just about as well as it is possible to do in words. However, I can't emphasize enough how difficult it is for all of us to realize the reality of the psyche, even though we talk about it all the time. And that's why Jung was so lonely. Intellectually it's easy enough to grasp the idea but to appreciate its living reality in our actual day-to-day life is quite another matter.

In order to illustrate this difficulty Jung was fond of recounting a situation where he had tried to impress upon a patient the reality of a psychic matter and he'd just get this blind, agreeable response which didn't seem to register the full reality. Jung said about this: "It was as if I were to tell that fellow that he has a rattlesnake in his pocket and he were to smile and say, 'Oh, is that so?' "

That's the nature of the reality of the psyche, and when it dawns on you, then it has the quality of a rattlesnake.

Now the reason we can't realize the reality of the psyche is that it requires a higher level of consciousness than we yet possess. It is my experience that only after years and years of analysis do a few people, a very few, begin to get a glimpse of it. But by and large it's not something available to our time. By and large it's a realization that's going to have to await future human development. And that's why Jung was so lonely.

He quotes the Church father Tertullian concerning the testimonies of the soul. (par. 556) I'm not going to read that because of its length, but I'm going to read a companion quote to it that is a kind of testimony to the reality of the psyche. This is a passage from the Gnostic teacher Monoïmos. It really points the way to a realization of that rattlesnake. Here's what he says:

> Seek him [God] from thyself, and learn who it is that takes possession of everything in thee, saying: *my* god, *my* spirit, *my* understanding, *my* soul, *my* body; and learn whence is sorrow and joy, and love and hate, and waking though one would not, and sleeping though one would not, and getting angry though one would not, and falling in love though one would not. And if you shouldst closely investigate these things, thou wilt find Him in thyself, the One and the Many, like to that little point, for it is in thee that he hath his origin.[31]

So here's something to meditate on: your thoughts, your feelings, your passions, your affects—they're *not yours at all*. You don't create them. It's only the child's psyche that thinks they are his. They come from an unknown source and flow through us and as the reality of the psyche begins to dawn then the objective realization also dawns that these constituents of the psyche are not created by the ego at all. The ego just notices that they've arrived, so to speak.

In continuing his remarks about the reality of the psyche Jung makes an important statement. He says, "Statements made in the Holy Scriptures are also utterances of the soul." (par. 557)

This is the methodological basis for all that follows in *Answer to Job* because Jung is taking scriptural material and interpreting and understanding that material as utterances of the soul—manifestations of the objective psyche. And the basis for Jung's assumption is that the Scriptures attain the designation of holiness or sacredness as a

---

[31] *Aion,* CW 9ii, par. 347.

judgment of the consensus. Over an adequate period of time the consensus of humanity, representing the collective psyche, acknowledges their numinosity and establishes them as having sacred content and thus marks them as the utterances of the soul.

And finally in *Lectori Benevolo,* Jung speaks about a dual standpoint toward the archetypal images, namely recognizing that they are both objects and subjects. That means that when we experience an archetypal image we can study it as an object—we can describe it, we can classify it. But at the same time it remains a subject. That means that the archetypal image is a separate personality. It's an interior personality that has something of its own subjective will and intention—which is what we would expect when we encounter an outer personality, an outer subject.

And since the archetypal image has this twofold reference then an encounter with such a content will have a twofold effect. It will affect me and I will affect it. When the ego encounters the archetype, the archetype is changed and when the archetype encounters the ego, the ego is changed. A double, reciprocal effect takes place.

Turning now to our third category, I asked you to reread the Book of Job in preparation for our study. Let me just remind you of the outline of the Job story.

There's a wager in heaven between Satan and Yahweh as to whether or not Job can be turned away from God—kind of a heavenly conspiracy. Job is then beset with multiple calamities. Job then questions his situation: "Why is this happening to me?" He calls out to God to explain to him why this is happening, to justify to him the reason for it. He says he's not an evil man and his life, his behavior, does not, in justice, warrant this kind of treatment. Counselors arrive on the scene who tell him, in effect, to quit questioning what's beyond him and just submit and admit that though he may not understand it, God is just. But Job refuses. He perseveres in his questioning and in maintaining his integrity, as he puts it. And then finally, Yahweh manifests. He shows himself in the whirlwind and in his great final speech says, in effect, "Who are you to question me? Look at all my grandeur." And with that, Job is silenced and accepts the situation. And Yahweh then restores all his property—better than before. That's the bare bones of the Biblical account.

Now this story is the prototype of what I call the Job archetype, which pictures a certain typical encounter between the ego and the Self. I distinguish four chief features of the Job archetype:

1) There's an encounter between the ego and the greater power.

2) A wound or a suffering of the ego results from the encounter.

3) The ego perseveres in insisting upon scrutinizing the experience in search of its meaning. It will not give up in despair or cynicism but perseveres in the assumption that the experience is meaningful. This corresponds to Jacob's refusal to release the angel that he's wrestling with until he receives a blessing. And this ego attitude corresponds also to Job's insistence on thinking that he knows that his redeemer lives—even though he's being mistreated.

4) As a result of that a divine revelation takes place by which the ego is rewarded with insight into the nature of the transpersonal psyche—and it will be an insight that satisfies the ego. It answers the question in some form or another and brings acceptance.

Now this full sequence can take place only if it isn't short-circuited by a personalistic or reductive interpretation at step three. You see, if Job had submitted to the advice of his counselors that some way or other he had it coming, even though he can't understand why, and he should admit that he's getting his just deserts, a short circuit would have taken place and there would have been no divine revelation.

This problem is illustrated by the dialogue that took place between Victor White and Jung. Victor White wrote a review of *Answer to Job*—a negative review, quite a negative review. I want to read you a little bit of that dialogue because it's so very relevant to the issues that *Answer to Job* confronts us with. I can't read you the whole thing, I don't have enough time, but I want to give you the flavor:

> Is it profitable, or even sensible to analyse a patient's gods without analysing the patient, or without even a glance at his case history? Can it be irrelevant to all that follows that, as the opening verses of the Book of Job tell us, Job is materially prosperous and spiritually complacent, that he "eschews" (the Hebrew means "turns aside from," "ignores') evil, that he is driving his children to drink, that he is anxiety-ridden with the suspicion that they precisely *blaspheme*. . . . Can we treat the archetypal antics as "autonomous," independently of Job's disturbed and anxious ego? And is it not sympto-

matic of the same split of ego from shadow that, as Job intensifies his repressions, his wife-anima is sick and tired of his infantile piety. . . . What lesson, as a pupil in psychology, am I supposed to derive from it all? That we can legitimately transfer our personal splits and ills to our gods and archetypes, and put the blame on them? . . . Or are the critics right who consider that Jungians have become so possessed by archetypes that they are in danger of abandoning elementary personal psychology altogether?[32]

Jung answered with this letter:

Now let us assume that Job is neurotic . . . he suffers from a regrettable lack of insight into his own dissociation. He undergoes an analysis of a sort, f.i. by following Elihu's wise counsel; what he will hear and what he will be aware of are the discarded contents of his personal subconscious mind. . . . You faintly insinuate that I am committing Elihu's error too, in appealing to archetypes first and omitting the shadow. *One cannot avoid the shadow* unless one remains neurotic. . . . The shadow is the block which separates us most effectively from the divine voice. . . .

If Job succeeds in swallowing his shadow he will be deeply ashamed of the things which happened. He will see that he has only to accuse himself, for it is his complacency, his righteousness, his literal-mindednes, etc. which have brought all the evil down upon him. . . . He will certainly fall into an abyss of despair and inferiority feeling, followed, if he survives, by profound repentance. He will even doubt his mental sanity: that he, by his vanity, has caused such an emotional turmoil, even a delusion of divine interference—obviously a case of megalomania.

After such an analysis he will be less inclined than ever before [to think] that he has heard the voice of God. Or has Freud with all his experience ever reached such a conclusion? If Job is to be considered as a neurotic and interpreted from the personalistic point of view, then he will end where psychoanalysis ends, viz. in disillusionment and resignation, where its creator most emphatically ended too.

Since I thought this outcome a bit unsatisfactory and also empirically not quite justifiable, I have suggested the hypothesis of arche-

---

[32] *Journal of Analytical Psychology,* vol. 4, no. 1 (January 1959), pp. 77ff (also quoted in Edinger, *The Creation of Consciousness: Jung's Myth for Modern Man,* pp. 77-78).

types as an answer to the problem raised by the shadow.[33]

You see, the problem raised by the shadow is this: if one takes it all personally, one falls into the abyss because the shadow has an archetypal dimension to it, and if you have to take complete responsibility for the shadow, that amounts to a total demoralization. Faced with the overwhelming force of the archetypal shadow, and understanding it as your complete responsibility, you have no alternative but to commit suicide.

Now these passages bring up a fundamental question that I want you to reflect on: In dealing with psychic problems in ourselves and in our patients, when is it proper to use a personalistic approach and when is it proper to use an archetypal approach? In other words, when is the Job archetype truly constellated and when can that symbolism be properly applied?

That's a question I'd like you to reflect on and perhaps some of you will have some comments and remarks, perhaps in the discussion or in the future. Because it's basic to our clinical work and to our own personal analysis.

---

[33] *Letters,* vol. 2, p. 545.

3
Paragraphs 560-576

Just as in a dream series one pays particular attention to the initial dream, in an important book one pays particular attention to the first sentence. Previously we discussed the title, the Prefatory Note and the *Lectori Benevolo* (To the Kind Reader), but today we begin our discussion of *Answer to Job* proper.

The initial sentence of *Answer to Job* is the following:

> The Book of Job is a landmark in the long historical development of a divine drama. (par. 560)

As I read that sentence I ask myself, "What does he mean, 'divine drama.' What's that?"

I think the term "divine drama" refers to the progressive, dramatic evolution and unfolding of the objective psyche in the course of emerging life, and in the course of human history. Actually this sentence could very well be translated a little differently. Translated as "historical development" is the word *Entwicklungswege,* which I think more literally might mean "process of evolution" or "path of evolution." *Entwicklung* is the word used for biological evolution, so it has a biological connotation in addition to a historical connotation. When we start to reflect on what's implied by this term, we have to look over the whole course of biological evolution, as we understand it.

Out of inorganic matter complex molecules somehow or other came together and developed the capacity to replicate themselves. Then they very gradually increased in their complexity until life forms arose and a whole process of increasing complexity unfolded until the incredibly rich panorama of vegetable/animal life as we know it came into being.

Somewhere in the course of that process came the momentous event when consciousness was born in our hominid ancestors. And then very gradually what we call the God-image started to emerge in a definite form, in definite images. It started with primitive animism, and then underwent progressive differentiation: from animal deities to matriarchal earth goddesses, to the sky gods of Mesopotamia and Ancient Greece, and finally to the monotheism of Yahweh worship. So as we look at that whole panorama we see a vast evolutionary unfolding of the divine drama—"divine" in the sense that it pertains to the transpersonal psyche—the objective psyche. This idea of a divine drama is totally missing from the scientific world-view, which is the predominant world-view today. It's heretical, according to the scientific world-view, to consider the possibility of purposefulness in the evolutionary sequence. That sort of thinking is not permitted. If you submit a paper to a scientific journal that contains that hypothesis—it won't get published.

The orthodoxy is that this has all taken place by chance, by random comings together, even though it patently defies common sense to imagine that chance phenomena can build up systems of greater and greater complexity. It violates the law of entropy, according to which random events level out, rather than increase in complexity. Nevertheless, that's the orthodoxy of the scientific world-view.

Opposed to that we have a rival orthodoxy: the anachronistic orthodoxy of what's called the creationists. This orthodoxy assumes that the story of Genesis is a literal fact, and it thereby provides the very thing that the scientific view lacks: an awareness of the divine drama. The trouble is, it's couched in literal, concretistic terms that do not fit the modern mentality.

So those are the two parties contesting this matter that Jung referred to in his Prefatory Note when he spoke about being torn apart by the two parties that contest this matter. Those are the representatives of the two parties.

A third view, which is based on an awareness of the reality of the psyche, allows the divine drama to reenter human awareness on a level, and with sufficient understanding, to do justice to both sides—to the core values of both sides.

Jung refers to this divine drama in a wonderful letter to Elined Kotschnig which I commend to you. I will read you a particular passage in which he refers to the divine drama. Jung is addressing the question of God's relationship to the world he has created:

When we consider the data of paleontology with the view that a conscious creator has perhaps spent more than a thousand million years, and has made, as it seems to us, no end of detours to produce consciousness, we inevitably come to the conclusion that—if we want to explain His doings at all—His behaviour is strikingly similar to a being with an at least very limited consciousness. Although aware of the things that are and the next steps to take, He has apparently neither foresight of an ulterior goal nor any knowledge of a direct way to reach it. Thus it would not be an absolute unconsciousness but a rather dim consciousness. Such a consciousness would necessarily produce any amount of errors and impasses with the most cruel consequences, disease, mutilation, and horrible fights, i.e., just the thing that has happened and is still happening throughout all realms of life.[34]

There's a little glimpse of Jung's overall view of the divine drama as it manifests in evolution and history. I have a fantasy on the subject myself that I'll read to you.

Suppose the universe consists of an omniscient mind containing total and absolute knowledge. But it is asleep. Slowly it stirs, stretches and starts to awaken. It begins to ask questions. What am I?—but no answer comes. Then it thinks, I shall consult my fantasy, I shall do active imagination. With that, galaxies and solar systems spring into being. Then the fantasy focuses on earth. It becomes autonomous, and life appears. Now the Divine mind wants dialogue and man emerges to answer that need. The deity is straining for Self-knowledge, and the noblest representatives of mankind have the burden of that divine urgency imposed on them. Many are broken by the weight. A few survive and incorporate the fruits of their divine encounter in mighty works of religion and art and human knowledge. These then generate new ages and civilizations in the history of mankind. Slowly, as this process unfolds, God begins to learn who He is.[35]

That's my image of the divine drama. You might reflect on the term and see what your image is of that process.

The second item I will discuss comes from paragraph 561 where Jung says:

---

[34] Ibid., p. 312.

[35] Edinger, *The Creation of Consciousness,* p. 56.

I shall not give a cool and carefully considered exegesis that tries to be fair to every detail, but a purely subjective reaction. In this way I hope to act as a voice for many who feel the same way as I do. . . . Even if we know by hearsay about the suffering and discord in the Deity, they are so unconscious, and hence so ineffectual morally, they arouse no human sympathy or understanding. Instead, they give rise to an equally ill-considered outburst of affect, and a smouldering resentment that may be compared to a slowly healing wound. And just as there is a secret tie between the wound and the weapon, so the affect corresponds to the violence of the deed that caused it.

"The affect corresponds to the violence of the deed that caused it." This means that our affects are the inner manifestions of Yahweh. Yahweh is the perpetrator of the deed that caused it, so the affect and its cause correspond to each other. *Our affects are the inner manifestations of Yahweh.* This is a crucial understanding. If you don't get this you will not understand *Answer to Job.* You won't be able to apply it in any personal or practical or genuine way. It will just remain an abstraction.

But this is very difficult to grasp, because we identify with our affects. We even call them ours—"my affect," "my anger," "my love." It would be more accurate to leave out the personal possessive pronoun. We tend to identify with our affects and so long as we do that we cannot see them objectively as objects. If I fall into a rage or a passion of any kind, in the terms of this book that we are studying, those phenomena are manifestations of Yahweh. That won't be hard for you to accept once you accept one other equation, namely Yahweh equals the unconscious. It won't be hard for you to accept that affects are products of the unconscious. We don't generate them—they happen to us. Yahweh = the unconscious. For the purpose of *Answer to Job,* that's the equation to keep in mind.

The third item concerns paragraph 562, which is a crucial paragraph and I'm going to quote it to you in its entirety. The first sentence needs to be changed because it's not translated quite accurately. You may think I'm nitpicking, but the statements are of such importance I think they should be precisely the way Jung put them. The first sentence should read as follows:

The Book of Job serves as a paradigm for a certain experience of God which has a very special significance for our time.

Jung continues:

> These experiences come upon man from inside as well as from out-
> side, and it is useless to interpret them rationalistically and thus
> weaken them by apotropaic means. It is far better to admit the affect
> and submit to its violence than to try to escape it by all sorts of in-
> tellectual tricks or by emotional value-judgments. Although, by giv-
> ing way to the affect, one imitates all the bad qualities of the outra-
> geous act that provoked it and thus makes oneself guilty of the same
> fault, that is precisely the point of the whole proceeding: the vio-
> lence is meant to penetrate to man's vitals, and he to succumb to its
> action. He must be affected by it, otherwise its full effect will not
> reach him. But he should know, or learn to know, what has affected
> him, for in this way he transforms the blindness of the violence on
> the one hand and of the affect on the other into knowledge.

I draw your attention again to that first sentence:

> The Book of Job serves as a paradigm for a certain experience of God
> which has a very special significance for our time.

A paradigm means a model to be used for guidance or imitation.
He's telling us then that Job and his suffering is a guiding model for
the sufferings of the modern ego. Here's the model for the process
of making suffering meaningful. I think one can say that every analysis that goes at all deep takes on the quality of the Job experience.
That's why I think of my little book on Blake's *Illustrations of the
Book of Job*[36] as a kind of portable analytic hour. It applies to every
life problem that one encounters, if one goes deeply enough—to the
core of it.

And I'd also draw your attention especially to the last sentence of
the paragraph:

> He should know, or learn to know what has affected him, for in this
> way he transforms the blindness of the violence on the one hand and
> of the affect on the other into knowledge.

This means that both Yahweh and the affect-laden ego are transformed by the conscious encounter between them, and by the perse-

---

[36] *Encounter with the Self: A Jungian Commentary on William Blake's*
Illustrations of the Book of Job.

vering effort to extract meaning from the experience. And to the extent that an individual finds the transpersonal meaning in the painful experience of the unconscious—to that extent he is contributing to the transformation of the God-image.

The fourth item comes from paragraph 567, where Jung says:

> This is perhaps the greatest thing about Job, that, faced with this difficulty [the awareness that Yahweh can be unjust], he does not doubt the unity of God. He clearly sees that God is at odds with himself—so totally at odds that he, Job, is quite certain of finding in God a helper and an "advocate" against God. As certain as he is of the evil in Yahweh, he is equally certain of the good. . . . He [Yahweh] is both a persecutor and a helper in one, and the one aspect is as real as the other. Yahweh is not split, but is an *antinomy*—a totality of inner opposites—and this is the indispensable condition for his tremendous dynamism. . . . Notwithstanding his wrath, Yahweh is also man's advocate *against himself* when man puts forth his complaint.

While keeping in mind our equation Yahweh = the unconscious, these statements about Yahweh may be applied to the nature of the unconscious. They are a description of the unconscious, which can cause terrible suffering—accidents and crippling symptoms of all kinds. We all know that, it's our work to deal with those things. And at the same time the unconscious is the source of transpersonal wisdom, support and guidance. It's the pathway to our being, to our wholeness.

As we know, the ego's attitude toward the unconscious largely determines the face that the unconscious will show to the ego, but one usually learns that only after being buffeted about quite a bit by this unconscious which is an antinomy.

The fifth item comes from paragraph 568. Jung speaks of Yahweh's "incalculable moods and devastating attacks of wrath." He continues,

> He had a *distinct personality,* which differed from that of a more or less archaic king only in scope.

This tells us that Yahweh is very much like an archaic king, so the unconscious is very much like an archaic king. We don't have archaic kings around any more, but we have their equivalents. We have dictators, we have Mafia bosses, we have petty tyrants of all kinds who rule their realms (whatever their realms may be) in the fashion of archaic kings. And we don't have to look only outside. Inside we don't have to go too far to discover the archaic king or queen who takes over when we are identified with the power motive.

One of the ways one can determine, one can study, phenomenologically, the nature of the unconscious Self is by observing individuals who are identified with the unconscious Self. These archaic kings among us are observable phenomena that reveal the nature of the unconscious Self to us.

The sixth item is also from paragraph 568, where Jung speaks about the difference between Yahweh and Father Zeus, who was detached and allowed the economy of the universe to run along pretty much on its own. He didn't demand much of anything from human beings except sacrifices because he didn't want anything from them, he had no plans for them. But Yahweh on the other hand was intensely interested in man because He needed them. So they are totally different personalities.

Jung isn't just indulging in some abstract observation about differing mythological figures. Remember that he is talking about psychology, so that the figure of Zeus and the figure of Yahweh will have their psychological references. Zeus and Yahweh were both sky gods, but Yahweh underwent a transformation and in his transformation he insisted on becoming the only god. Zeus was part of a polytheistic arrangement and he was perfectly happy with that. But Yahweh could not tolerate that situation—as illustrated by his very first commandment, "You shall have no gods except me."

This is a huge transformation in the God-image between the polytheistic Zeus and the monotheistic Yahweh. It represents the difference between the *Iliad* and the Exodus. The *Iliad* pictures human existence as a brutal, tragic drama in which mankind is caught in the conflict between deities. That's the cause of the Trojan War, because if the deities are at war with each other then man has to act out that divine conflict. It's an unrelieved tragedy. Whereas the Exodus pictures human existence as a redemption drama of cooperation between the one God and his selected human beings who worship him.

These distinctions still exist today. The Homeric polytheism of the *Iliad* and the basic psychology pictured by that work—I think that corresponds to the psychology of our neighborhood gangs. Every now and then a gang member encounters a fundamentalist Christian and is converted and leaves his gang psychology, he leaves the *Iliad* and goes to the Exodus. His God-image undergoes transformation. That's an example of how that transformation of the God-image which is enshrined in our literary heritage still lives itself out today.

The seventh item comes from paragraph 569, where Jung speaks about the covenant that was developed between Yahweh and certain individuals, and how the Eighty-ninth Psalm pictured that covenant as broken. The Eighty-ninth Psalm first quotes Yahweh as having said to David:

> I have made a covenant with my Chosen,
> I have given my servant David my sworn word:
> I have founded your dynasty to last for ever,
> I have built you a throne to outlast all time.

The psalm continues for some verses to praise God and then the Psalmist reminds Yahweh of his statement,

> I will not break my covenant,
> I will not revoke my given word;
> I have sworn on my holiness, once for all,
> and cannot turn liar to David.
>
> *
>
> And yet you have rejected, disowned
> and raged against your anointed;
> You have repudiated the covenant with your servant
> and flung his crown dishonored to the ground.
>
> You have pierced all his defenses
> and laid his forts in ruins.[37]

This is the same psalm that a certain great Rabbi of Spain was said to have been unable to read because it saddened him so much.[38]

Commentators generally connect the Eighty-ninth Psalm with the

---

[37] Jerusalem Bible.

[38] *See Aion,* CW 9ii, par. 169.

destruction of Israel in 587 B.C. and the Babylonian Exile. That is what the psalmist is referring to when he accuses Yahweh of breaking the covenant with David. That was the supreme catastrophe for ancient Israel. The destruction of Jerusalem and the subsequent Babylonian captivity seemed to contradict all of Yahweh's promises.

Individuals encounter similar events in their lives when they feel that everything they have had faith in has been thrown into question. What happens in such a case is that the individuals in their anguish and inability to accept the catastrophe ask again and again the question, "Why did this happen to me? Why did God permit this terrible thing to happen?"—this accident, this illness, this loss of a loved one—this catastrophe, whatever it is.

There are five possible answers to that question. One of them is *"God has punished me for my sins."* If you are aware of your sins and accept the event as punishment, then that satisfies you, that's your meaning. That's the "Jeremiah reaction." That's what Jeremiah told Israel: the reason this happened to you is that you're being punished for your sins.

Another possible reaction is that *"I'm the victim of Satan, the Evil one, who is responsible."* That's the dualistic or Manichean reaction, it sees the world as engaged in a conflict between two different deities: the Good and the Evil.

The third possibility is that *"This catastrophe is actually good for me in some higher way I can't understand."* I call that the Apostle Paul reaction. He said, "All things work together for good to them that love God"[39]—if you can see far enough. It usually takes some faith to assume that one.

The fourth possibility is that the suffering is caused by chance, because there is no transpersonal agency in human affairs. *"God doesn't exist, or if he does exist he doesn't concern himself with man."* That's the secular reaction. It doesn't offer much comfort but if you believe it you can harden yourself and adopt a stoic attitude.

The fifth possibility is the one Jung has discovered, namely, *"God is an antinomy who isn't quite conscious of what he is doing."* That's the Job reaction, Job who knows that his redeemer lives and

---

[39] Rom. 8:28, Authorized Version.

who says to God, "Though you kill me, yet will I trust in you."[40]
Job also realizes that by having that awareness about God he is contributing to God's transformation.

That's the Job reaction and it's one that never existed before in
human thought until Jung interpreted it in that way.

---

[40] Job. 13:15, Authorized Version (paraphrase).

4

Paragraphs 577-608

First we have an item left over from last time.

In paragraph 574 Jung says:

> The character thus revealed fits a personality who can only convince himself that he exists through his relation to an object. Such dependence on the object is absolute when the subject is totally lacking in self-reflection and therefore has no insight into himself. It is as if he existed only by reason of the fact that he has an object which assures him that he is really there.

And then on into the next paragraph where he makes the following remarks:

> Existence is only real when it is conscious to somebody. That is why the Creator needs conscious man even though, from sheer unconsciousness, he would like to prevent him from becoming conscious. And that is also why Yahweh needs the acclamation of a small group of people. One can imagine what would happen if this assembly suddenly decided to stop the applause: there would be a state of high excitation, with outbursts of blind destructive rage, then a withdrawal into hellish loneliness and the torture of non-existence, followed by a gradual reawakening of an unutterable longing for something which would make him conscious of himself.

This is a magnificent description of a basic feature of the unconscious, namely its need to be seen. This is the basic work of analysis: to pour attention into the unconscious so that it can be seen. And as it is seen, it is appeased. The outbursts of blind, destructive rage are assuaged when it is seen. As was mentioned in the discussion period last time, this description is very similar to what's spoken of in clinical terms as narcissism. In *The Creation of Consciousness* I report a dream that actually makes that connection explicit. This is a dream a man had right after reading *Answer to Job:*

> I see a huge ape-like man without a neck. His huge head is attached directly to his shoulders. He is naked and is looking lasciviously at a

42

woman. I feel that he must be trained, so I ask him to put on his clothes. He expels flatus loudly and leaves the room.[41]

The dreamer associated the ape-like man with the description of Yahweh in *Answer to Job* and also to an autistic child of his acquaintance. Infantile and child autism is a kind of extreme or pure example of the narcissistic syndrome. The dream here is picking up and equating a certain aspect of the Yahweh phenomenon with autism, which is total preoccupation with one's inner center—the Self. The whirling motion that is so characteristic of autistic children is expressive of the fact that they are living completely within the confines of identity with the Self. So they're revolving around that inner center. In another dream that I quote on the same page, an ape-like figure is again associated with the God-image.

If you recognize the narcissistic propensity to be an indication that the Yahweh God-image is activated, then you pour attention into that image but at the same time you recognize that a distinction should be made between the ego and the God-image. When narcissism (so-called) is disentangled from the ego it takes on a totally different quality. If you separate it from its identification with the ego, then that so-called narcissism becomes the demand of the God-image for attention. Then it is no longer the ego's demand for attention, but rather the demand of the Self for attention, and that changes the whole state of affairs.

I'm now turning to tonight's material. I have a number of items to refer to—nine, if I get to them all. The material in this book is just loaded with profound psychological insights that are embedded in it, providing you make the translation from the mythological imagery that Jung is using to the psychological correlates. You then begin to appreciate the powerful insights present in *Answer to Job*. I'm going to try to point out a few of those to you.

First, in paragraph 577:

The special providence which singled out the Jews from among the divinely stamped portion of humanity and made them the "chosen people" had burdened them from the start with a heavy obligation.

---

[41] *The Creation of Consciousness,* p. 76.

This is the theme of the Chosen One. It is really a central theme of individuation and I draw your attention to a fine essay on the subject by Rivkah Kluger in her book *Psyche and Bible*. It's an essay on the chosen people. I would like to take a lot of quotes from this because she has some marvelous insights. Let me mention a couple to give you the flavor of it. I hope you will then look it up for yourself and read it at your leisure.

> Because Yahweh is himself holy, singled out from all the other gods, the people, correspondingly, must be holy. The God Yahweh, grown together as it were out of many polytheistic god-figures into one God-*personality* and having thereby become *distinct,* chooses for himself a people equally distinct as his vis-á-vis. Projected onto a people as a collective individual we see here the birth of the idea of the individual, that is, one who steps out of the anonymity of the cycle of nature into a personal, unique fate.[42]

One other one:

> Returning to our initial question, why God chose one single people, we see from the inner dynamics of the total election event that it *had* to be *some* people. . . . That it was *Israel* may be related to its difficult situation, which prepared it to follow an *inner* way. It was a poor peasant people, eternally oppressed by the surrounding great kingdoms, Egypt and Babylon. It could make room for itself only inwardly, and was thereby peculiarly suited to take upon itself the misery and dignity, the curse and blessing, of God's election. [And here's quite an insightful remark:] It was, so to speak, *God's easiest prey.*[43]

Now these remarks are all profoundly relevant to the experience of the ego as it encounters the Self and becomes aware that it is the one uniquely chosen to incarnate the Self. To be chosen is often experienced as having been the easiest prey—as being the outcome of a state of misery. Being chosen doesn't come out of a state of fullness, it comes out of a state of emptiness.

Item 2, par. 579:

> Yahweh abandons his faithful servant to the evil spirit and lets him

---

[42] *Psyche and Bible,* p. 25.
[43] Ibid., p. 41.

fall without compunction or pity into the abyss of physical and moral suffering. From the human point of view Yahweh's behaviour is so revolting that one has to ask oneself whether there is not a deeper motive hidden behind it. Has Yahweh some secret resistance against Job? . . . But what does man possess that God does not have? Because of his littleness, puniness, and defencelessness against the Almighty, he possesses, as we have already suggested, a somewhat keener consciousness based on self-reflection: he must, in order to survive, always be mindful of his impotence. God has no need of this circumspection, for nowhere does he come up against an insuperable obstacle that would force him to hesitate and hence make him reflect on himself.

Now here's another crucial insight about the nature of psychology. What he is telling us is that the experience of weakness or defeat is a sine qua non for consciousness. You cannot be a conscious being unless you can experience weakness and defeat. I talk about that whole matter in *Ego and Archetype,* where I used a diagram to illustrate the psychic life cycle (see next page).[44]

What it pictures is the way consciousness is progressively developed out of the original condition of ego/Self identity. The original condition is inflation. The infantile psyche is in a state of identification with the Self and it is in a state of inflation. It is identified with the Deity. Very progressively, if life provides the right lessons through rejections and defeats and experiences of weakness, it gradually becomes conscious. And you go through that cycle again and again and each time it goes around there's a little increase in consciousness.

The psychology of the spoiled child short-circuits this cycle. The child's ego/Self identity goes uncorrected. It acts out the inflation and instead of being punished or defeated, it is allowed to get away with it so that the cycle does not complete itself.

This cycle pictures the transformations that take place as ego/Self identity is subjected to recurrent experiences of defeat, failure and weakness. That composite entity of ego and Self undergoes transformation. This means that as consciousness grows, both the ego

---

44 *Ego and Archetype: Individuation and the Religious Function of the Psyche,* p. 41.

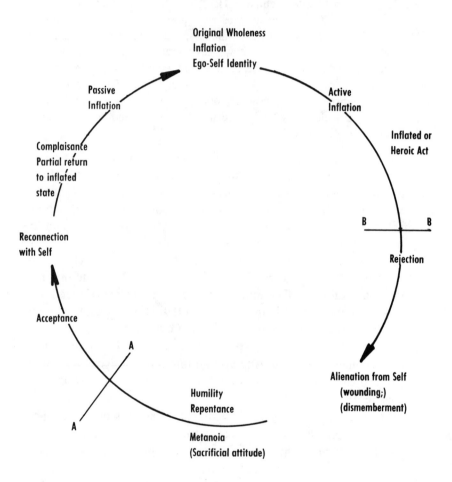

The Psychic Life Cycle

and the Self undergo transformation. In terms of Job and Yahweh it would mean that as Job's consciousness of Yahweh's nature grows, Yahweh is transformed.

It is a real disadvantage to be omnipotent, to be immortal. In fact, as far as I can tell, consciousness can only develop in mortal creatures. I don't believe it's possible for consciousness to develop in immortal creatures, if there be such a thing. In other words, the archetypes themselves cannot evolve into full consciousness without being routed through a mortal ego to bring that consciousness into realization. That is what Jung is saying here, in effect, when he says that Job possesses something God does not have.

Item 3 comes from paragraph 583:

> Why Job's torments and the divine wager should suddenly come to an end is not quite clear. So long as Job does not actually die, the pointless suffering could be continued indefinitely. We must, however keep an eye on the background of all these events: it is just possible that something in this background will gradually begin to take shape as a compensation for Job's undeserved suffering.

The key word here is compensation. You have heard that term before I'm sure—"compensatory function of the unconscious," for example. What Jung is alluding to here is the profound psychological law that when the ego becomes too one-sided, weighted too much in one direction, the unconscious psyche then constellates the contrary in the unconscious to balance the one-sidedness. So here that process of compensation is occurring within the God-image, the Yahweh figure himself.

> It is just possible that something in this background will gradually begin to take shape as compensation for Job's undeserved suffering.

What that means is that injustice, especially if it is consciously perceived, constellates its correction in the other—in the unconscious or in the outside world. In other words, *injustice consciously perceived and borne constellates justice.* This is really quite a fundamental psychological law.

I would like to draw your attention to a wonderful essay on this subject by Emerson. It's entitled "Compensation." He had a wonderful intuitive perception of how the compensatory process operates in the collective psyche. To give you a taste of it:

> Thus is the universe alive. All things are moral. . . . Justice is not
> postponed. A perfect equity adjusts its balance in all parts of life.
> . . . Take what figure you will, its exact value, nor more, nor less,
> still returns to you. Every secret is told, every crime is punished,
> every virtue rewarded, every wrong redressed, in silence and certainty.
> What we call retribution is the universal necessity by which the
> whole appears wherever a part appears.[45]

That's an insight which is not visible if you look at the way the
world functions on the surface. But if you perceive how it functions
from the inside, it's a profound truth.

> All things are double, one against another—Tit for tat; an eye for an
> eye; a tooth for a tooth; blood for blood; measure for measure; . . .
> Give and it shall be given you. . . . Curses always recoil on the head
> of him who imprecates them.[46]

So he reaches the conclusion then:

> A wise man will . . . know that it is the part of prudence to face ev-
> ery claimant and pay every just demand on your time, your talents,
> or your heart. Always pay.[47]

The idea is that since the compensatory balance exists, if you
don't pay voluntarily, it will be extracted from you involuntarily and
it is really much more agreeable to do it voluntarily.

> The benefit we receive must be rendered again, line for line, deed for
> deed, cent for cent, to somebody. Beware of too much good staying
> in your hand. It will fast corrupt and breed worms. Pay it away
> quickly.[48]

That's the idea of compensation, and how every extreme or one-
sided state of affairs rights itself through the action of the unconscious.

Item 4 comes from paragraph 584. Jung says:

---

[45] *Essays,* p. 99.

[46] Ibid., p. 106.

[47] Ibid., p. 109.

[48] Ibid., pp. 109-110.

Job realizes God's inner antinomy, and in light of this realization his knowledge attains a divine numinosity.

What does he mean, "his knowledge attains a divine numinosity"? I would suggest that what he is referring to here is actually an experience of the *coniunctio*. If Job's knowledge, his consciousness, attains a divine numinosity, that means he's become a partner in Yahweh's divinity. The realization that is being expressed here is that of the ego/Self partnership—their partnership in creating consciousness. It is that realization which conveys meaning to Job's experience and amounts to an experience of justification. He is justified, through his awareness that his experience is part of the ego/Self partnership which provides him with a role in the divine drama. The divine drama, you remember, was the term that appeared in the first sentence of the book.

Item 5, paragraph 587:

[Yahweh] pays so little attention to Job's real situation that one suspects him of having an ulterior motive which is more important to him.

And then comes the crucial sentence:

Job is no more than the outward occasion for an inward process of dialectic in God.

Now here is another very profound idea. Let me restate it in psychological terms: *The ego is the outward occasion for an inward process of dialectic in the Self.*

So here again we have the realization of a partnership. Once again such a realization communicates a sense of meaningfulness, because the painful experience that one is going through is purposeful. It is part of a larger transpersonal process. It is part of the divine drama, the process of inner dialectic in God which requires an ego for that process to proceed.

Item 6, paragraph 591:

Yahweh sees something in Job which we would not ascribe to him but to God, that is, an equal power which causes him to bring out his whole power apparatus and parade it before his opponent. Yahweh projects on to Job a sceptic's face which is hateful to him because it is his own, and which gazes at him with an uncanny and critical eye. He is afraid of it, for only in face of something frightening does one let off a cannonade of references to one's power, cleverness, courage, invincibility, etc.

And then in paragraph 594 Jung adds:

Job is challenged as though he himself were a god.

This continues to emphasize the theme I have already underscored: the theme of ego/Self partnership. It seems that the ego carries divine or God-like attributes when it is participating in the inner dialectic of the God-image. It then takes on a certain numinosity. What that means, if you think it through, is that everything that pertains to the ego—the earthy, the particular, the dark, everything which establishes the individual as something definite and unique—all of these earth attributes are imbued with a certain divine numinosity. You see what a radical transformation of viewpoint that represents as contrasted with the earlier one-sided spiritual viewpoint, where all that pertained to the earth was thought of as just something to be purified and removed.

Item 7 comes from paragraph 595:

The conflict becomes acute for Yahweh as a result of a new factor.
. . . something that has never occurred before in the history of the world, the unheard-of fact that, without knowing it or wanting it, a mortal man is raised by his moral behaviour above the stars in heaven, from which position of advantage he can behold the back of Yahweh, the abysmal world of "shards."

According to the Cabala, the original divinity was just a point, the so-called *En Soph.* From it emanated the original First Man, who then differentiated himself into the ten sefiroth, the so-called sefirotic tree. According to the Cabalistic symbolism, in the formation of the sefirotic tree the primordial light was poured into the vessels or shells of the ten sefiroth. The first three held the light, but the lower seven could not endure the pressure of the light that was poured into them, and they broke.

This is what's called the breaking of the vessels. What was created then were a lot of broken pieces, the so-called shards. These shards, according to the Cabalistic speculation, then took on the quality of evil, and became the depth of the great abyss in which the spirit of evil dwells. It's a symbolic image, one of its features is that as the godhead manifests itself, as it emanates and tries to differentiate itself, it splits. It undergoes a *separatio* process and part of it breaks up into an evil world, the abysmal world of shards. That's what Jung refers to in this passage.

Item 8 is referred to in paragraph 600:

Unconsciousness has an animal nature. . . . This [animal] symbolism explains Yahweh's behaviour, which, from the human point of view, is so intolerable: it is the behaviour of an unconscious being who cannot be judged morally. Yahweh is a *phenomenon* and as Job says, "not a man."

Then I draw your attention to the remarkable footnote 13:

The naive assumption that the creator of the world is a conscious being must be regarded as a disastrous prejudice which later gave rise to the most incredible dislocations of logic.

Jung goes on to say in this footnote that when we understand that what we are dealing with is "divine unconsciousness and lack of reflection," then we are enabled to form "a conception of God which puts his actions beyond moral judgment and allows no conflict to arise between goodness and beastliness."

What Jung is describing here is the nature of the unconscious. This is not metaphysical theology that he is indulging in, it is empirical psychology. Jung is describing what he knows from his own experience.

Item 9 comes from paragraphs 605 and 606. He tells us there that Job did get his satisfaction:

Nevertheless, Job got his satisfaction, without Yahweh's intending it and possibly without himself knowing it. . . . Yahweh's allocutions have the unthinking yet nonetheless transparent purpose of showing Job the brutal power of the demiurge: "This is I, the creator of all the ungovernable, ruthless forces of Nature, which are not subject to any ethical laws. I, too, am an amoral force of Nature, a purely phenomenal personality that cannot see its own back."

This is, or at any rate could be, a moral satisfaction of the first order for Job, because through this declaration man, in spite of his impotence, is set up as a judge over God himself.

Jung puts this idea even more clearly in the form he expressed it to Rivkah Kluger, who passed it on to us in her book, *Satan in the Old Testament.* Here's what she has Jung say about Job's satisfaction:

> In his great final speech God reveals himself to Job in all his fright-fulness. It is as if he said to Job: "Look, that's what I'm like. That is why I treated you like this." Through the suffering which he inflicted upon Job out of his own nature God has come to this self-knowledge and admits, as it were, this knowledge of his frightfulness to Job. *And that is what redeems the man Job.* This is really the solution to the enigma of Job, that is a true justification for Job's faith, which, without this background, would, in its cruelty and injustice, remain an open problem. Job appears here clearly as a sacrifice, but also as the carrier of the divine fate, and that gives meaning to his suffering and liberation of his soul.[49]

What makes this statement so relevant for us in our psychological work is that it is a symbolic description of the consciousness of the transpersonal dimension of an ordeal, a problem, or an experience of personal suffering. This is the consciousness which redeems the suffering, which redeems the complex. It is a symbolic description of the dawning of a transpersonal dimension of consciousness that has the power of redemption.

---

[49] *Satan in the Old Testament,* p. 129.

5
Paragraphs 609-624

Before I begin there's a correction to the text of *Answer to Job* that I want to point out. The first sentence of paragraph 616 should start, "Not from mere thoughtlessness . . ."

I have seven items I want to comment on tonight. The first is the most substantial. It concerns the figure of Wisdom, to whom Jung introduces us here. This is a major archetypal image, so it's something you should be thoroughly familiar with in order to recognize her when she shows up in dreams. I want to summarize briefly her historical evolution.

Just as we can consider Yahweh to be the masculine personification of the collective unconscious, so we can consider Wisdom to be the feminine personification of the collective unconscious. Where she appears most prominently in the text she carries three chief names which I have placed on the board. I employ the original languages because the unconscious loves ancient languages. Jung was well aware of that fact. That's one major reason that you find so much Greek and Latin in Jung's work. That was his way of conveying that fact to us.

Sophia is her Greek form, *Chochma* is her Hebrew form, and *Sapientia Dei* is her Latin form. She shows up first in Greek philosophy where we might place her more or less arbitrarily at about 600-300 B.C. She is really the central image of Greek philosophers, so they even name themselves "Lovers of Sophia." They think of themselves as her lovers, and that is the word then that passed on into the Greek scriptures and into the Gnostic literature, the term Sophia.

Later she is discussed in Proverbs which Jung quotes. Proverbs is a composite collection. Chapters 1 to 9, in which she is described, could perhaps be tentatively dated somewhere around 400 B.C., maybe a little earlier. Let's examine her self-description:

> I, Wisdom, dwell with experience and judicious knowledge. Mine are counsel and advice. Mine is strength, understanding. By me kings reign and lawgivers establish justice. By me princes govern and no-

bles, all the rulers of the earth. Those who love me I also love, and those who seek me find me. With me are riches and honor. My fruit is better than gold. On the way of duty I walk, along the paths of justice. The Lord begot me, the first-born of his ways, the forerunner of his prodigies of long ago. From of old I was poured forth. When there were no depths I was brought forth, when there were no fountains or springs of water, before the mountains were settled into place. When he established the heavens I was there, when he made firm the skies above, when he fixed fast the foundations of the earth; when he set for the sea its limit so that the waters should not transgress his command; then I was beside him as his craftsman. I was his delight, day by day, playing before him all the while, playing on the surface of his earth; and I found delight in the sons of men.[50]

Along about the same time comes the Song of Songs, dated somewhere between 500-400 B.C. Wisdom is not specifically referred to there, but the Shulamite is later identified with Sophia, so for that reason the Song of Songs becomes a major Wisdom text. The whole drama of the Shulamite and her lover corresponds to the perpetual loveplay of the *hieros gamos* between Yahweh and Sophia.

Next in time comes Ecclesiasticus, which is also called the Wisdom of Jesus Ben Sirach. That is one of the books of the Apocrypha. It's found in the Greek Hebrew scriptures and that's one of the advantages of using either the Jerusalem Bible or the New American Bible. Because they are Catholic versions they include the Apocrypha. Ecclesiasticus we can date to approximately 200 B.C. Wisdom is discussed chiefly in chapters 1, 4 and 24. Jung quotes one passage from chapter 24 in which Wisdom associates herself with a tree. Another passage of Ecclesiasticus that I am particularly fond of is found in chapter 4, where we read:

> Wisdom instructs her children
>> and admonishes those who seek her.
> He who loves her loves life;
>> those who seek her out win her favor.
> He who holds her fast inherits glory;
>> wherever he dwells, the Lord bestows blessings.

---

50 Prov. 8:12-31, New American Bible (condensed).

Those who serve her serve the Holy One;
  those who love her the Lord loves.
He who obeys her judges nations;
  he who harkens to her dwells in her innermost chambers.
If one trusts her he will possess her;
  his descendents too will inherit her.
She walks with him as a stranger,
  and at first she puts him to the test;
Fear and dread she brings upon him
  and tries him with her discipline;
With her precepts she puts him to the proof,
  until his heart is fully with her.
Then she comes back to bring him happiness
  and reveal her secrets to him.[51]

The next Wisdom text is the Wisdom of Solomon. Sometimes it is just called Wisdom. This is another of the books of the Apocrypha. This one dates back to about 50 B.C.

In her is a spirit, intelligent, holy, unique, manifold, subtle, agile, clear, unstained, certain. Loving the good, keen, unhampered, beneficent, kindly, firm, secure, tranquil, all-powerful, all-seeing, and pervading all spirits though they be intelligent, pure and very subtle. For wisdom is mobile beyond all motion, and she penetrates and pervades all things by reason of her purity. She is an aura of the might of God. She who is one can do all things and renews everything while her self perduring; and passing into holy souls from age to age she produces friends of gods and prophets.[52]

Next in this unfolding in time comes the Gnostic literature which we can date approximately from 100-300 A.D. According to this literature Sophia is one of the aeons in the pleroma, who falls into matter. She becomes enamored of matter and succumbs to its embrace and then has to be rescued. The legend of the Gnostic Simon Magus is a kind of prototype. According to that legend Simon Magus discovered Sophia reincarnated as a version of Helen of Troy in a brothel in Tyre. That is how she had fallen into matter. He rescued her from the brothel in Tyre and made her his partner. What we have

---

51 Eccles. 4:11-18, New American Bible.
52 Wisd. of Sol. 7:22-27, New American Bible (condensed).

there is an amalgam of the divine Sophia on the one hand, and Helen of Troy on the other. What that legend actually does is to unite the two strains of scripture, the Greek and the Hebrew. The Greek scripture, of course, was the *Iliad* in which Helen of Troy was a central figure.

Then medieval philosophy picked up the figure of what it now called *Sapientia Dei*. She became a major figure around which speculation gathered. She was considered to be the eternal form out of which God created the world. So she embodied all the eternal Platonic ideas out of which the world was created.

Then finally comes Sophia or *Sapientia* as she appeared in alchemy. You may remember from the *Mysterium* class[53] that we had a text involving the Shulamite, "dark but comely," and she was asking to be rescued. She was the personification of the *prima materia,* seeking rescue by the alchemists. That's another version of Sophia caught in the dark embrace of matter, requiring rescue. The outstanding alchemical example of Sophia or *Sapientia Dei* text is the *Aurora Consurgens,* which Marie-Louise von Franz edited and to which she contributed a commentary. I consider *Aurora Consurgens* von Franz's finest work. Let me read you just a paragraph of her commentary. The whole alchemical text concerns the *Sapientia Dei* and its redemption. Here is the way von Franz begins:

> The first chapter introduces a mystical female figure who appears at first as the personified *Sapientia Dei*. . . . This feminine divine hypostasis is painted on a broad canvas, and is amplified by numerous Biblical sayings and comparisons. At first it's the same personification we see in Proverbs, Ecclesiasticus and Wisdom of Solomon. In patristic literature she was mostly interpreted as Christ, the pre-existent Logos or as the sum of the eternal forms of the "self-knowing primordial causes," exemplars or prototypes in the mind of God. She was also considered the *archetypus mundus,* "that archetypal world, after whose likeness this sensible world was made" and through which God becomes conscious of himself. *Sapentia Dei* is thus the sum of archetypal images in the mind of God.[54]

---

[53] [Edinger's course on Jung's *Mysterium Coniunctionis* (CW 14) is available on audio tape from the C.G. Jung Institute of Los Angeles.—Ed.]

[54] *Aurora Consurgens,* pp. 155f (modified slightly).

That's a brief summary of how Sophia has appeared in the collective Western psyche in its traditional material.

Item 2 comes from paragraph 616 of *Answer to Job:*

From the ancient records we know that the divine drama was enacted between God and his people, who were betrothed to him, the masculine dynamis, like a woman, and over whose faithfulness he watched jealously.

We have here the image of Yahweh as the husband and Israel as the wife. Job then becomes the individual personification of Israel and Yahweh treats Job the way a jealous husband treats a wife, putting her to the test to see if she really is faithful to him. This brings up a whole series of analogies between the image of the marriage relationship and the ego/Self relation. Yahweh is husband and Israel is wife. Israel is functioning then as a kind of collective ego, and Yahweh represents the Self.

You may remember from *Aion* that Jung stated that the anima or animus can be realized only through a relation to a partner of the opposite sex, because only in such a relation do their projections become operative. The same idea can be applied to the psychology of Yahweh as Jung traces it. He had a consort, his consort was Sophia, but he forgot about her or more precisely he never really knew her. Just as the ego, in order to become conscious of the contrasexual other, must experience a real encounter with the opposite sex through a relationship, so must Yahweh do the same in order to become conscious of his other. Because Yahweh is eternal and immortal his other is temporal and mortal. *He needs that other in order to become conscious of his inner contrary.*

As we reflect on the implications of this analogy between the marriage relationship and the relationship between the ego and the Self, we then realize that Jung's fine essay "Marriage As a Psychological Relationship"[55] can be transferred almost in its entirety to the ego/ Self relationship. Nearly everything he says about marriage as a psychological relationship applies also to the relation between the ego and the Self. Jung says that at the beginning of such a relationship there is a high degree of unconscious identification between the part-

---

[55] In *The Development of Personality,* CW 17, pars. 324-345.

ners and only very gradually does the relationship evolve into a relation between separate conscious individuals. He says that seldom or never does a marriage develop into an individual relation smoothly or without crisis. There is no birth of consciousness without pain. Those are Jung's words.

Certainly the same thing applies to the ego/Self relation. One has to go through experiences of divorces and alienations and losses of connection to the God-image in order for the ego's relation to the Self to finally evolve into something conscious rather than something unconscious, that is, a state of ego/Self identity.

There's another idea which I think is particularly productive and helpful that Jung elaborates in his essay on marriage as a psychological relationship. That's the idea of the container and the contained. He says that in every relationship one of the partners will be more or less contained in the other. Let me read a few remarks he makes about this phenomenon, because this particular concept I think is an important tool in our analytic understanding:

> The one who is contained feels himself to be living entirely within the confines of his marriage; his attitude to the partner is undivided.
> . . . The unpleasant side . . . is the disquieting dependence upon a personality that can never be seen in its entirety.[56]

That is from the point of view of the contained one.

The container, on the other hand, Jung says, will miss all the subtleties and complexities that would correspond to his own facets, and he is both disturbing to the other's simplicity and also is left dissatisfied because his complexity cannot be mirrored by the simplicity of the contained one.

Jung continues:

> The simpler nature works on the more complicated one like a room that's too small, that does not allow him enough space. The complicated nature, on the other hand, gives the simpler one too many rooms with too much space, so that she never knows exactly where she really belongs.[57]

---

[56] Ibid., par. 332.

[57] Ibid., par. 333. [R.F.C. Hull, translator of the original German, writes in

Then Jung goes on to say it usually happens that sooner or later the one functioning as the container, who is dissatisfied, starts looking around, looks out the window to see if he might find somebody so that he, too, could find some containment.

That all applies to the ego/Self relation. The ego of course is the smaller, simpler, contained entity, and the Self is the container. As long as that situation prevails, then a Job event will never happen because he will hearken to his counselors. The counselors express the state of containment, and that is what they informed Job: "You are smaller than Yahweh, so you are the contained one—accept that situation." It is because Job did not accept it that to some extent he turned the tables on Yahweh and in one respect, for a moment at least, the ego became the container and the Self the contained.

Item 3 derives from paragraph 616, where Jung says that Yahweh

projects his own tendency to unfaithfulness upon a scapegoat. There is reason to suspect that he is about to loosen his matrimonial ties with Israel but hides this intention from himself.

Yahweh, like a jealous husband, is preoccupied with the possibility of his wife's infidelity. That state of affairs is illustrated very vividly in the third chapter of Jeremiah. This is Yahweh speaking:

If a man sends away his wife and, after leaving him, she marries another man, does the first husband come back to her? Would not the land be wholly defiled? But you have sinned with many lovers, and yet you would return to me! says the Lord. Lift your eyes to the heights, and see where have men not lain with you? By the waysides you waited for them like an Arab in the desert. You defiled the land by your wicked harlotry. Therefore the showers were withheld, the spring rain failed. But because you have a harlot's brow you refused to blush.[58]

The Lord said to me in the days of King Josiah, "See now what rebellious Israel has done. She has gone up every high mountain and

---

a footnote that for the sake of clarity he assumed the container—and the "complicated nature"—to be the man and the contained—the "simpler nature"—to be the woman: "This assumption is due entirely to the exigencies of English grammar, and is not implied in the German text. Needless to say, the situation could just as easily be reversed."—Ed.]

[58] Jer. 3:1-3, New American Bible.

under every green tree she has played the harlot. And I thought after she had done all this she will return to me. But she did not return. Then, even though her traitor sister Judah saw that for all the adulteries rebellious Israel had committed, I put her away and gave her a bill of divorce, nevertheless her traitor sister Judah was not frightened; she too went off and played the harlot. Eager to sin, she polluted the land, committing adultery with stone and wood."[59]

It's laid out very explicitly. In our clinical terminology Yahweh has an infidelity complex. We encounter this situation (it is not so uncommon) where a husband or a wife becomes convinced that the spouse is being unfaithful. Jung tells us the reason for that in paragraph 620:

> Yahweh had lost sight of his pleromatic coexistence with Sophia since the days of the Creation. Her place was taken by the covenant with the chosen people, who were thus forced into the feminine role.

What Yahweh is doing is entertaining the prospect of being unfaithful to Israel in order to have a relation with Sophia. But from what was said earlier we can consider that his relation with Israel (a kind of projection of the feminine consort) was a necessary step in Yahweh's becoming conscious of Sophia. Just as the human male ego must integrate the anima via projection, via an experience with a living partner of the opposite sex, so Yahweh must also have that experience, must have the external love relationship with Israel, and then later withdraw the projection. The infidelity complex is a kind of unconscious expression of the fact that he's going to turn from a projected relationship to his consort to a conscious, direct relationship to Sophia herself. That anticipated infidelity is then projected upon Israel.

The same thing applies to the individual caught in the infidelity complex. What is called for is the realization that the individual does indeed need to be partially "unfaithful" to the external partner in order to have a relationship with the inner consort—the anima or animus. And believe me, that is often experienced by the partner as an infidelity.

Item 4 comes from paragraph 617:

---

[59] Jer. 3:6-9, New American Bible.

Whoever knows God has an effect on him.

This sentence epitomizes the entire book. It is the most important single sentence in the book. And for that reason I've put it up on the board in German to emphasize Jung's original formulation, *"Wer Gott erkennt, wirkt auf ihn."*

I don't think we can overestimate what a revolutionary and profound fact and discovery is expressed by this simple sentence. I think this is how psychotherapy works. As the analyst comes to know the nature of the unconscious of the patient, as the analyst is able to perceive the abysmal world of shards that resides in the unconscious of the patient, as the analyst is able to get behind it, so to speak—to see it—that act of having-been-seen has an effect. Naturally it is our task to communicate verbally what we see to the patient, but even in the absence of an explicit communication the having-been-seen acts on the unconscious of the patient.

I won't ask you to take that as dogma, I ask you to take it as an hypothesis and consider it in your work and see if it is verified. I think very often it is. Of course naturally we can't verify it all the time because sometimes the mills of God grind rather slowly. But it's a very important principle of developing consciousness. Also I think this insight is of such fundamental importance to the collective that this single sentence is enough to create a whole new aeon—the Jungian aeon.

Item 5 comes from paragraph 619:

> If the original father Adam is a copy of the Creator, his son Cain is certainly a copy of God's son Satan, and this gives us good reason for supposing that God's favourite, Abel, must also have his correspondence in a "supracelestial place."

The idea here is that Adam, as a prototype of the ego, is made in God's image and therefore if Adam had two sons that means (if he's following the divine pattern) that Yahweh also had two sons. It is Jung's point that only one son became visible at first, the Cain son, namely Satan. But the Abel son is going to show up shortly, the Christ son.

Another parallel between Yahweh and Adam is that they both had two wives. In the same paragraph, Jung says:

The original man who was created in the the image of God had, according to tradition, two wives, just like his heavenly prototype.

Yahweh's two wives are Israel and Sophia. Just as the Self has two wives, the ego has two wives. I think what that refers to is this: the two wives of the ego are the outer partner and the inner partner. We often encounter a situation where a man is caught between two women, or a woman is caught between two men. There is a certain kind of psychology that is chronically getting into triangles of that sort. One way we describe it in a man is as a split anima. Another way to describe it is as an exteriorization of the two wives archetype. One of those two wives belongs inside and when one is inside, then one on the outside suffices. But when a person is in the process of discovering the inner one, it very often happens that life gets complicated with two outer wives because the unconscious inner wife is projected outward.

The same thing applies then to the Self. The Self has two wives. The ego is the outer wife of the Self and the eternal consort is the inner wife of the Self. That would correspond in Biblical terminology to Israel as the outer wife of Yahweh and Sophia as the inner consort of Yahweh.

6

Paragraphs 625-648

There are two items left over from last time that I want to talk about. In paragraph 621 Jung says:

> At the bottom of Yahweh's marriage with Israel is a perfectionistic intention which excludes that kind of relatedness we know as "Eros." The lack of Eros, of relationship to values, is painfully apparent in the Book of Job.

And then again, in paragraph 623:

> God was now known, and this knowledge went on working not only in Yahweh but in man too. Thus it was the men of the last few centuries before Christ who, at the gentle touch of the pre-existent Sophia, compensate Yahweh and his attitude. . . . [Sophia or Wisdom] shows them the bright side, the kind, just and amiable aspect of their God.

The idea here is that Job's seeing of Yahweh has the effect of Yahweh's discovering his missing Eros. This is an example of the statement we discussed last time, "Whoever knows God has an effect on him." Job's knowledge of God has the effect of making God conscious of the relatedness principle, because someone found him out in a state of unrelatedness and perceived that condition. That perception itself had the effect of correcting the situation.

We must always ask ourselves, with these mythological statements that Jung makes, "What does this mean in practical, psychological terms?" That's what we have to deal with in our daily life. One thing I think it means is that consciousness of the violent, unrelated power aspect of the unconscious transforms it. I believe this process takes place both in regard to one's *self*-knowledge, in which one observes the violent power aspect of one's own unconscious, and I believe it operates also in relation to the knowledge of others.

The analyst observes the violent power aspect of the patient's unconscious in the same way as Job observed it with Yahweh. That very observation promotes a transformation—subtly but nonetheless in a very real way. Once the unconscious has been seen and recognized by someone for what it is, that event constellates a need for it to change.

The second item left over from last time is referred to in paragraph 624, where Jung says:

> The reappearance of Sophia in the heavenly regions points to a coming act of creation. She is indeed the "master workman"; she realizes God's thoughts by clothing them in material form, which is the prerogative of all feminine beings. Her coexistence with Yahweh signifies the perpetual *hieros gamos* from which worlds are begotten and born. A momentous change is imminent: God desires to regenerate himself in the mystery of the heavenly nuptials.

The key phrase here is "the perpetual *hieros gamos* from which worlds are begotten and born." We must ask ourselves what does that mean? What is the perpetual *hieros gamos*? *Hieros gamos* means sacred marriage. It is an image of *coniunctio*. I understand "the perpetual *hieros gamos*" to refer to the bedrock foundation of the objective psyche, the collective unconscious. Jung tells us that Job's encounter with Yahweh had the effect of constellating or activating or bringing into visibility the perpetual *hieros gamos*, which then led to the transformation of Yahweh.

I think something analogous took place in connection with Jung's experience of the perpetual *hieros gamos*. He describes that experience in *Memories, Dreams, Reflections*. It took place during his illness in 1944. Let me read some selected phrases:

> Everything around me seemed enchanted. . . . I myself was, so it seemed, in the Pardes Rimmonim, the garden of pomegranates, and the wedding of Tifereth with Malchuth[60] was taking place. Or else I was Rabbi Simon ben Jochai whose wedding in the afterlife was being celebrated. It was the mystic marriage as it appears in the Cabbalistic tradition. I cannot tell you how wonderful it was. . . . There followed the Marriage of the Lamb, in a Jerusalem festively bedecked. . . . These were ineffable states of joy. . . . the *hieros gamos* was being celebrated. . . . All-Father Zeus and Hera consummated the mystic marriage, as it is described in the *Iliad.*[61]

---

[60] Two of the sefiroth of the sefirotic tree. See above, p. 505.
[61] *Memories, Dreams, Reflections,* p. 294.

This was Jung's experience of what he here calls the perpetual *hieros gamos*. The fruit that was born out of Jung's experience was, in quick succession, *The Psychology of the Transference, Aion, Answer to Job* and *Mysterium Coniunctionis*. This fruit is an example of the "worlds that are begotten and born" out of the "perpetual *hieros gamos*" referred to in paragraph 624. Over and beyond that, it's my opinion that the universal fruit of Jung's experience of the perpetual *hieros gamos* was the birth of the new Jungian aeon, which those four books describe.

Now to today's assignment.

> Just as the decision to become man apparently makes use of the ancient Egyptian model, so we can expect that the process itself will follow certain prefigurations. (par. 625)

> As nothing can happen without a pre-existing pattern, not even creation *ex nihilo,* which must always resort to the treasure-house of eternal images in the fabulous mind of the "master workman," the choice of a model for the son who is now about to be begotten lies between Adam . . . and Abel. (par 641)

What I want to call your attention to is the unqualified statement that *"nothing can happen without a pre-existing pattern."* It is very instructive to observe how Jung elaborates his argument about the process of God's incarnating as man. He emphasizes right at the start that even God has to have a pre-existing pattern. That shows you what vital importance Jung attaches to psychic patterns of structure as the basic elemental requirements for any psychic operation.

This is a very important principle to apply in the course of practical analysis. As we listen to patients and study their unconscious material we must always be on the alert for the basic patterns that are being revealed to us. Those would be the very things that the patient misses entirely. The patient is at sea in a chaos of events, but if we are familiar with the basic psychic patterns, we will perceive them and can point them out. There will be, by and large, two different levels on which these patterns will be based.

First there will be psychological material derived chiefly from the *personal* level—from personal childhood experience. This material will reveal repetitions of the patterns of experience that were laid down in childhood: the particular family constellations and the particular experiential constellations that imprinted themselves on the child's psyche and will remain there for all time. Analysis does not erase those childhood patterns; the most it can do is to make them conscious.

Second, below that personal level of patterning will be the *collective* level, where we perceive the archetypal patterns. The personal patterns that we detect on the basis of childhood experience also will have their archetypal prototypes. When the time has come for the patient to engage the archetypal dimension of the life patterns he is involved with, the dreams will indicate that fact by taking on an archetypal quality. That will then encourage us to shift the interpretation of patterns from the personal to the archetypal level. As Jung tells us here, God himself is dependent on pre-existing patterns whenever he wants to create something. Jung could hardly state more emphatically how crucially important he considers the basic typical patterns of the psyche to be.

In the following paragraph Jung talks about the fact that Yahweh is obliged to incarnate. The incarnation is only partially consummated, however, because both mother and son are not completely human since they don't have the full quota of human sinfulness. Then in paragraph 627 he goes on to say:

> This arrangement, though it had the effect of exalting Mary's personality in the masculine sense by bringing it closer to the perfection of Christ, was at the same time injurious to the feminine principle of imperfection or completeness, since this was reduced by the perfectionizing tendency to the little bit of imperfection that still distinguishes Mary from Christ. *Phoebo propior lumina perdit!* [Phoebus, the sun, destroys lights near to it.] Thus the more the feminine ideal is bent in the direction of the masculine, the more the woman loses her power to compensate the masculine striving for perfection, and a typically masculine, ideal state arises which, as we shall see, is threatened with an enantiodromia. No path leads beyond perfection into the future—there is only a turning back, a collapse of the ideal, which could easily have been avoided by paying attention to the feminine ideal of completeness.

This way of putting it is, I think, an interesting variation from the usual descriptions of the nature of the masculine and feminine principles—it helps us see the contrast between those two principles from a slightly different angle. The masculine spirit principle is striving for perfection and the feminine nature or relatedness principle is striving for completeness. Here again, I think an awareness of this particular pair of contrasting entities is very helpful in the analytic process. Certainly in the modern situation the tendency to perfection has gotten far more attention than the tendency to completeness. We are all very alert to the idea of introducing the completeness principle as a way of mitigating a one-sided emphasis on perfection.

But at the same time we must not forget that we encounter a fair number of individuals who are more complete than they are perfect. I mean by that a very unconscious completeness. Nature is complete. She's all of one piece, but all of her contrasts operate quite outside any consciousness. It is not uncommon that an inchoate, undifferentiated psychology that can claim a certain kind of unconscious, undifferentiated completeness needs to be confronted with the goal of perfection. These are a pair of opposites, each of which has an equal right to exist, and the question for the therapist is which way to lean with any particular individual and set of circumstances.

In paragraph 629 Jung makes a very obscure and esoteric remark. Listen to this carefully, because what Jung is doing in this work perhaps above all others is speaking to us from a level of consciousness of which we have almost no awareness at all. We really have to strain ourselves to grasp what it is he is talking about.

Although the birth of Christ is an event that occurred but once in history, it has always existed in eternity. For the layman in these matters, [and who isn't a layman?] the identity of a nontemporal, eternal event with a unique historical occurrence is something that is extremely difficult to conceive. He must, however, accustom himself to the idea that "time" is a relative concept and needs to be complemented by that of the "simultaneous" existence, in the Bardo or pleroma, of all historical processes. What exists in the pleroma as an eternal process appears in time as an aperiodic sequence, that is to say, it is repeated many times in an irregular pattern. . . . When these things occur as modern variants, therefore, they should not be regarded merely as personal episodes, moods, or chance idiosyncrasies in people, but as fragments of the pleromatic process itself, which, broken up into individual events occurring in time, is an essential component or aspect of the divine drama.

Now that's quite a mouthful. One of the key terms he uses here is "pleroma." That's a Gnostic term that refers to the eternal realm outside of phenomenal, temporal existence. It means approximately the same thing as the collective unconscious. I think we need to practice a certain kind of visualization of the collective unconscious. Because it is not tangible and visible most people do not even acknowledge its existence.

We who know that it exists, by virtue of our experience of it, need to practice or exercise our visualization of what our experience of the collective unconscious indicates that it is. I would suggest that we think of it as a very subtle fluid that pervades everything. It is most concentrated in human beings but it is not at all confined to them. We know through our experience of synchronicity[62] that it extends all the way down to inorganic matter.

I think we have to hypothesize that the fluid pervades all of existence as we perceive it. It means, then, that the basic patterns that go to make up existence are pervasive and repeat themselves on all levels, not only on the psychological level but also on the chemical and physical and astronomical levels. On all those levels the same patterns repeat themselves. The energy, the dynamism that operates through that fluid, likewise extends like a pervasive network through everything, and that all goes to make up what's called the pleroma. But it exists outside of time and space. Things get a little hard to visualize when you add that proviso, but it is a necessary proviso because our experience teaches us that the collective unconscious does transcend time and space. Time and space are categories of the ego so they are necessary for ego consciousness but they do not apply to the unconscious.

What Jung is saying here then is that these archetypes, these *entia* in the pleroma are eternal entities that erupt into the temporal process. They erupt into individual ego consciousness because the temporal

---

[62] Meaningful coincidence, as for instance between a dream and an outer event. See "Synchronicity: An Acausal Connecting Principle," *The Structure and Dynamics of the Psyche*, CW 8, pars. 816-968.

process derives from ego consciousness. On such occasions the ego is caught in a piece of the divine drama and lives it out, more or less consciously or unconsciously.

Another way of putting it is that the ego is in time and the Self is in eternity. The ego is the agent of the Self in time, so to speak. When certain archetypal entities erupt into ego existence, then it is the task of the ego to embody those entities, incarnate them, and realize them as consciously as possible. If there is little consciousness attached to the event, then the ego becomes the tragic victim of the archetype that it is constellating. If there is more consciousness involved, then the ego does not have to be a tragic victim because it knows what is happening to it. It behaves in a much different way and can mediate the archetypal pattern much differently.

In paragraph 634 Jung says that Yahweh makes the mistake of not consulting his omniscience. Jung writes:

> We can only explain this on the assumption that Yahweh was so fascinated by his successive acts of creation, so taken up with them, that he forgot about his omniscience altogether. It is quite understandable that the magical bodying forth of the most diverse objects . . . should have caused God infinite delight. . . .

And in paragraph 635:

> The Book of Job still rings with the proud joy of creating.

And 636:

> So even in Job's day Yahweh is still intoxicated with the tremendous power and grandeur of his creation.

Speaking of basic patterns, here is one such pattern, intoxication with creativity. Jung talks about this from another angle in his Zarathustra seminars. It is a particularly fine passage that I've already quoted in another place, but I want to repeat it to you because it is so very relevant:

> [The creative forces] have you on the string, and you dance to their whistling, to their melody. But inasmuch as you say these creative forces are in Nietzsche or in me or anywhere else, you cause an inflation, because man does not possess creative powers, he is possessed by them. . . .

Nietzsche of course could not help looking at the thing and then he was overwhelmed with resentments because the creative powers steal your time, sap your strength. . . . Therefore, such people feel so terribly cheated; they mind it, and everybody ought to kneel down before them in order to make up for that which has been stolen by God. The creative forces have taken it out of them, and therefore they would like to personify them, to imagine that they are Shiva, in order to have the delight of being creative. But if you know you are creative and enjoy being creative, you will be crucified afterwards, because anybody identified with God will be dismembered. An old father of the church . . . said that . . . [our] creative spirit can penetrate the depths or the heights of the universe like God . . . but on account of that he will also have to undergo the divine punishment. That would be the dismemberment of Dionysos or the crucifixion of Christ.[63]

This is what happens to the individual who identifies with creativity. It is an intoxication of delight while at the same time it is followed by dismemberment. It is striking how these remarks of Jung's also apply to his description of Yahweh. He is telling us that Yahweh is intoxicated by his creativity, that he is identified with it. But then what happens is that he has to undergo crucifixion as Christ. The pattern applies to Yahweh as well as to man.

Paragraph 639:

There can be no doubt that he [Yahweh] did not immediately become conscious of the moral defeat he had suffered at Job's hands. In his omniscience, of course, this fact had been known from all eternity, and it is not unthinkable that the knowledge of it unconsciously brought him into the position of dealing so harshly with Job in order that he himself should become conscious of something through this conflict, and thus gain new insight.

Here is an important idea, that whenever one finds himself in a state of conflict with someone or with a situation, he should entertain the hypothesis that the psyche has propelled him into that situation in order to generate consciousness. That is an almost infallible law. If you entertain that hypothesis you will find it confirmed almost every

---

[63] *Nietzsche's* Zarathustra: *Notes of the Seminar Given in 1934-1939,* vol. 1, pp. 57-58 (also quoted in Edinger, *Anatomy of the Psyche,* p. 64).

time. The outer person or event that one is in conflict with is an exteriorization of an inner antagonist, and as one pays attention to that possibility the outer conflict resolves because it has become internalized and one has all he can handle taking care of what is going on inside.

The major theme of this assignment is the idea of God's becoming man. In paragraph 640, Jung says:

> Yahweh must become man precisely because he has done man a wrong. . . . Because his creature has surpassed him he must regenerate himself.

And in another place, paragraph 631:

> One should make clear to oneself what it means when God becomes man. It means nothing less than a world-shaking transformation of God. It means more or less what Creation meant in the beginning, namely an objectivation of God.

We can go in a lot of different directions with this very profound, many-faceted symbol of the incarnation of God or of God's becoming man. One direction I want to take with it is that I see it as referring to the humanization of the unconscious on all levels. The unconscious is not human. The personal unconscious is infantile. The collective unconscious is animal, or inorganic, or divine.

So what does it mean then for the collective unconscious to become man? I think it means approximately the same thing as is meant by the symbolic image of the alchemists who created a homunculus—a little man—in their retort. They turned the *prima materia* into a homunculus which was one of the symbols of the Philosophers' Stone. In other words, they turned base matter into something human, something man-like. It means something like the humanization of the universe, or the humanization of reality.

Remember that Jung states that Job discovered that Yahweh is a phenomenon and not a man. Elsewhere he tells us that God is reality itself (par. 631). If God has become man, then reality itself has been humanized. It means that reality itself takes on a human face, has become friendly to man rather than being the brute, indifferent nature that we perceive it to be. This is the implication of the alchemical term that I have placed on the board, *salvator macrocosmi*. One of the symbols of the Philosophers' Stone is the *salvator macrocosmi,* the Savior of the Universe. That is the meaning of that term. And it contrasts with the other term, *salvator microcosmi* which was applied to Christ, who was called the Savior of Man, the little universe, the microcosm.

Christ was understood theologically to have come to save man from the world. The effect then of Christian theology is to pluck man right out of the world, as if to say, "Get out of this vale of tears as quickly as you can and get up to heaven." That is the way man is saved. But the world is left behind, to its own devices. The Philosophers' Stone of the alchemists, on the other hand, is the savior of the world—it is the savior of the universe. This means essentially the same thing as Jung is talking about when he speaks of the requirement for Yahweh to become man because Job has seen him.

7

Paragraphs 649-661

Item 1 is found in paragraph 650, where we read:

[Satan's] comparative ineffectiveness can be explained on the one hand by the careful preparations for the divine birth, and on the other hand by a curious metaphysical phenomenon which Christ witnessed: he saw Satan fall like lightning from heaven. In this vision a metaphysical event has become temporal; it indicates the historic and—so far as we know—final separation of Yahweh from his dark son. Satan is banished from heaven. . . . Although he is banished from the heavenly court he has kept his dominion over the sublunary world [the earth]. He is not cast directly into hell, but upon earth.

What I am concerned with here is the image of a spiritual or angelic being falling out of heaven and down to earth. This is a fundamental image that one finds scattered in various places in the Scriptures. It also often comes up in dreams. It has a twofold meaning in accordance with the twofold nature of the image: (1) Satan's banishment from heaven and (2) his falling to earth.

It refers, as Jung says, to a decisive *separatio* within the Godhead. The Yahwistic and the Satanic aspects of the Godhead are sundered. Satan is kicked out of heaven. It represents a decisive separation of the opposites: of good from evil and of heaven from earth. So Yahweh now becomes identified with heaven and spirit, and Satan becomes identified with earth and matter. That is one psychological reference.

There are other examples of this image. For instance in the twelfth chapter of Revelation, which we will be studying soon, we read:

Woe to the inhabitors of the earth and of the sea! for the devil is come down unto you, having great wrath, because he knoweth that he hath but a short time.[64]

That is an event that is supposed to happen at the end of the

---

[64] Rev. 12:12, Authorized Version.

Christian aeon. Then there is another reference to this same image in the sixth chapter of Genesis:

> The sons of God saw the daughters of men that they were fair; and they took them wives. . . . The sons of God came in unto the daughters of men, and they bare children to them.[65]

Here again we have the image of angels—angelic beings, called the sons of God—who are lured to earth by the daughters of men, and who are then called the fallen angels. Those fallen angels then teach humanity the arts and sciences. We will be reading the Book of Enoch next week in which there is a lengthy description of this event—how the fallen angels teach man the arts and sciences.

In addition to the *separatio* factor, the other major meaning is that it represents *coagulatio.* I consider the details of this image in *The Anatomy of the Psyche.*[66] The idea of a descent from one level to another belongs to the symbol system of *coagulatio,* another word for which is incarnation. When something descends from an upper spiritual level to a lower realm, it takes on body as it descends. That is the process of *coagulatio.* It is the descent of heavenly spiritual stuff that falls into matter. A Gnostic example of this image is Sophia, who out of desirousness for the image that she sees reflected in the lower material realms, falls into the embrace of matter and undergoes incarnation. This is another image of *coagulatio,* of the process of a spiritual content undergoing embodiment.

All of this has to do with ego development. In this symbolism, that which pertains to earth and body and matter refers to the ego—it is the ego then that is the incarnating agent, and realizes or gives body or real fleshly existence to psychic stuff that is just abstract until it's lived out concretely in the personal life of a particular ego.

Another interesting image that fits this same pattern is Lucifer's fall from heaven as described in Milton's "Paradise Lost." I think it is probably significant that that particular classic was written in the seventeenth century, just as we had entered into the final quarter of the Christian aeon. Let me read you a few lines about when Lucifer rebels against God and is expelled from heaven, just in the same

---

[65] Gen. 6:2,4, Authorized Version.

[66] Chapter 4, pp. 83-116.

fashion that the image of Satan is expelled from heaven:

> He trusted to have equal'd the Most High,
> If he oppos'd; and with ambitious aim
> Against the Throne and Monarchy of God
> Rais'd impious War in Heav'n and Battel proud
> With vain attempt. Him the Almighty Power
> Hurl'd headlong flaming from th'Ethereal Skie
> With hideous ruin and combustion, down
> To bottomless perdition, there to dwell
> In Adamantine Chains and penal Fire,
> Who durst defie th'Omnipotent to Arms.[67]

That's an image of ego development!

Item 2 is from paragraph 651:

> But although Christ has complete confidence in his father and even feels at one with him, he cannot help inserting the cautious petition—and warning—into the Lord's Prayer: "Lead us not into temptation, but deliver us from evil." God is asked not to entice us outright into doing evil, but rather to deliver us from it. The possibility that Yahweh, in spite of all the precautionary measures and in spite of his express intention to become the Summum Bonum, might yet revert to his former ways is not so remote that one need not keep one eye open for it.

I thought this would give me an opportunity to say a few words about the psychological implications of the passage that we know of as the Lord's Prayer. This comes from the sixth chapter of Matthew. Let me remind you of how it goes:

> Our Father who art in heaven, hallowed be thy name. Thy kingdom come, thy will be done on earth as it is in heaven. Give us this day our daily bread and forgive us our trespasses [or debts] as we forgive those who trespass against us, and lead us not into temptation but deliver us from evil. . . .

That prayer has been on the lips of millions and millions of individuals at the times of greatest crisis. It is laden with psychological impact. It is divided into seven "petitions." (Jung speaks of the sixth petition as the words "lead us not into temptation.") When looked at

---

67 "Paradise Lost," book 11, lines 40-49.

psychologically you see right away that it is a formula for maintaining a connection between the ego and the Self. Let me just illustrate that briefly with each of these seven petitions.

Petition 1. "Hallowed be thy name," or "Thy name be sacred." That means I must remember the transpersonal sacred dimension of life. That is what the ego is reminding itself—to remember that life is not just secular, it has a transpersonal dimension.

Petition 2. "Thy kingdom come." The ego here is announcing that it recognizes that the rule of the Self should prevail.

Petition 3. "Thy will be done on earth as it is in heaven." Here the ego is saying, "I am going to live my life out of the same rule that you bring to your kingdom."

Petition 4. "Give us our daily bread." (The Vulgate says, "Give us our supersubstantial bread," which I think puts a nice angle onto it.) The idea there would be a petition or request for the inflow of nourishing images and meaning which is the psychological bread.

Petition 5. "Forgive us our trespasses," or "our debts." I prefer "trespasses" (though debts is the more common translation) because it emphasizes the nature of the ego's sin against the Self. Its characteristic sin is the inflation of identifying with the Self—in other words, trespassing on the Self's territory.

Petition 6. "Lead us not into temptation," is the one Jung refers to, because the fact is that the Self in its desire for total realization, total incarnation of its opposite nature, leads one into evil as well as into good. It is quite understandable that that petition would be included.

Petition 7. "Deliver us from evil." Protect us from disruptive dangers that you cannot help but lead us into.

Item 3 is brought up in paragraph 655:

> When Christ leaves the earthly stage, he will ask his father to send his flock a Counsellor (the "Paraclete") who will abide with them and in them forever. The Counsellor is the Holy Ghost, who will be sent from the father. This "Spirit of Truth" will teach the believers "all things" and guide them "into all truths." According to this, Christ envisages a continuing realization of God in his children, and consequently in his (Christ's) brothers and sisters in the spirit.

What Jung is referring to comes from the fourteenth and sixteenth chapters of John. Let me read parts of both, because this image of the coming of the Paraclete is another very important psychological symbol for our understanding. Christ is here announcing that he is going to die shortly, and he is informing his disciples of that fact, and telling them not to be disturbed because there is going to be a replacement. This is from the Jerusalem translation:

> It is for your own good that I am going, because unless I go the Advocate [the Paraclete], will not come to you; but if I do go, I will send him to you.[68]

> I shall ask the Father and he will give you another Advocate [Paraclete] to be with you forever, that Spirit of truth, whom the world can never receive, since it neither sees nor knows him, but you know him, because he is with you, he is in you. I will not leave you orphans. I will come back to you. In a short time the world will no longer see me, but you will see me, because I will live and you will live. On that day you will understand that I am in my Father, and you in me, and I in you.[69]

What does this mean? It means that a literal, concrete embodiment of the Self for a given person—which is the role Christ was fulfilling for his disciples at the time—that that concrete, literal embodiment must die in order for the ego/Self relation to be internalized.

The coming of the Paraclete we can understand clinically as an image of the resolution of the archetypal transference. Thus, at the conclusion of an analysis, when the issue of the resolution of the transference is uppermost, the analyst must convey precisely the same message: "I must go and it is to your advantage that I go and unless I go your direct inner relation to the Self cannot appear." And in order to promote that inner direct relation to the Self we have to encourage active imagination. In the later phases of analysis active imagination is the primary agency for the resolution of the transference. Active imagination is the evocation of the Paraclete.

Item 4, paragraphs 657 and 658, concerns a really crucial theme, the continuing incarnation. This idea is the core of the Jungian myth:

> God's Incarnation in Christ requires continuation and completion because Christ, owing to his virgin birth and his sinlessness, was not

---

68 John 16:7.
69 John 14:16.

an empirical human being at all. As stated in the first chapter of St. John, he represented a light which, though it shone in the darkness, was not comprehended by the darkness. He remained outside and above mankind. Job, on the other hand, was an ordinary human being, and therefore the wrong done to him, and through him to mankind, can, according to divine justice, only be repaired by an incarnation of God in an empirical human being. This act of expiation is performed by the Paraclete; for, just as man must suffer from God, so God must suffer from man. Otherwise there can be no reconciliation between the two.

The continuing, direct operation of the Holy Ghost on those who are called to be God's children implies, in fact, a broadening process of incarnation. Christ, the son begotten by God, is the first-born who is succeeded by an ever-increasing number of younger brothers and sisters.

This is the idea of the continuing incarnation. It's another expression of the process of individuation but it's a more vivid, more evocative symbol for the process of individuation which otherwise has a rather abstract quality about it. Jung says more about this theme later on in *Answer to Job,* but I first want to read you part of a letter he wrote to Elined Kotschnig. I would like to remind you that this letter, written in English, is a major text of the new Jungian myth.

The significance of man is enhanced by the incarnation. We have become participants of the divine life and we have to assume a new responsibility, viz. the continuation of the divine self-realization, which expresses itself in the task of our individuation. Individuation does not only mean that man has become truly human as distinct from animal, but that he is to become partially divine as well. This means practically that he becomes adult, responsible for his existence, knowing that he does not only depend on God but that God also depends on man. Man's relation to God probably has to undergo a certain important change: Instead of the propitiating praise for an unpredictable king or the child's prayer to a loving father, the responsible living and fulfilling of the divine will in us will be our form of worship of and commerce with God. His goodness means grace and light and His dark side the terrible temptation of power.[70]

---

[70] *Letters,* vol. 2, p. 316.

Item 5, paragraph 658:

The agonizing death of his [Yahweh's] son is supposed to give him satisfaction for an affront he has suffered, and for this "moral injury" he would be inclined to take a terrible vengeance. Once more we are appalled by the incongruous attitude of the world creator towards his creatures, who to his chagrin never behave according to his expectations. It is as if someone started a bacterial culture which turned out to be a failure. He might curse his luck, but he would never seek the reason for the failure in the bacilli and want to punish them morally for it. Rather, he would select a more suitable culture medium.

That particular image of trying to understand God's relation to man through man's creation of a bacterial culture has a very interesting parallel in a science-fiction story by Stanislav Lem who is a particularly fine science-fiction author. He's written a story called "Non Serviam," which is Latin for "I may not serve."

In this story a scientist creates a computer world in which conscious beings exist within the computer context. What he calls personoids. And these entities, as they gain consciousness, begin to indulge in metaphysical speculation about the nature of their creator. And they divide up into various factions. The two chief factions are the Godlies and the Ungodlies. Their question was does their creator want them to believe in him and would he punish them if they don't believe in him? They begin a dispute. A split develops between the two. One side assumes that the creator God requires reverence, love and devotion, and in order to win salvation one must be grateful to the maker for creating him and do one's best to serve God. The other side thinks—not at all. We must assume God is just and omniscient. Nothing whatever is demanded because a God that craves such feeling—of being loved and served—must first of all assure his creatures that he actually exists. He can't require them to rely on speculation about his existence. If he's almighty he could have provided certainty and since he did not provide it (assuming he exists) he must not have thought it necessary. And if he's not almighty would he be deserving of such feelings and service at all? So that particular view says, no, we're not obliged to serve this God (who probably doesn't exist anyway) because the fact that he doesn't demonstrate his existence to us means we're under no obligation to serve him.

To the scientist who's been listening in on all this (and realizes they're talking about him) this last reasoning seems incontrovertible:

> I'm the creator and I did produce that world with the aid of Adonai 9 computer program and the fact is that I have not communicated to them either my existence or anything about my existence. And they arrived at that idea only by inference and I do not at all feel myself entitled to demand of them any particular privileges—love, gratitude or even services. Even though I'm omnipotent with regard to their world—I can pull the plug on them any day—I don't even love them, actually.[71]

I'm going into this because it illustrates an issue the modern mind is engaged with. Science-fiction is right on the border of science, where imagination and science meet. It's a place where the collective unconscious has a chance to speak to the modern world, and we discover in stories of this sort how the same matter that Jung is dealing with, on a far deeper level, is also engaging the collective psyche.

Item 6 comes from paragraph 659:

> The fact that Christian ethics leads to collisions of duty speaks in its favour. By engendering insoluble conflicts and consequently an *afflictio animae*, it brings man nearer to a knowledge of God. All opposites are of God, therefore man must bend to this burden; and in so doing he finds that God in his "oppositeness" has taken possession of him, incarnated himself in him. He becomes a vessel filled with divine conflict.

I just wanted to draw your attention to that stunning statement because it concerns a basic issue we're dealing with all the time, both in ourselves and in our patients—the matter of the opposites. Jung is emphasizing here that the experience of the conflict of the opposites is an experience of God who is being incarnated in his oppositeness. This, needless to say, adds a whole level of understanding to the experience of conflict.

Item 7, paragraph 660, is a deep one:

> Because the *imago Dei* pervades the whole human sphere and makes mankind its involuntary exponent, it is just possible that the four-hundred-year-old schism in the Church and the present division of the

---

[71] "Non Serviam," in *A Perfect Vacuum*, p. 195 (modified).

political world into two hostile camps are both expressions of the unrecognized polarity of the dominant archetype.

The basic axiom here is that "the *imago Dei* pervades the whole human sphere and makes mankind its involuntary exponent." I prefer a slightly different translation of that sentence (which hinges on how you translate the verb *darstellen*): "The *imago Dei* pervades the whole human sphere and is involuntarily represented by mankind."

I hope you realize what this sentence implies. I want to say a bit about what I think it implies. You remember I mentioned before that you can think of the collective unconscious as a very subtle fluid pervading all of the universe but being especially concentrated in the psyche of humanity. This corresponds to the image of the alchemical *elixir permanens*. It's the fluid that permeates everything. It can seep its way into everything. And *that's* the word Jung uses here: "The *imago Dei* PERVADES the whole human sphere."

The God-image *(imago Dei)*, therefore, as the core archetype of the collective unconscious, is the central agent and creative authority which determines the functioning of all individuals and all organic groupings of individuals. And by organic groupings I mean all families, tribes, factions, parties, religions, nations—all groupings, small or large, which are unified by mutual identification with an origin, a cause or a creed. These origins, causes and creeds will be expressions of the God-image which is the operative central agent in the psyche of that particular group. What that means then is that in all conflicts between nations, creeds—different factions of all kinds—each side will be acting out of a commitment to its own version of the God-image. In other words, the conflict between any two factions is a conflict within the God-image itself.

I hope you all follow that. If not we'll go over it further in the discussion period. But this is my effort to elaborate what is condensed in this one sentence, "The *imago Dei* pervades the whole human sphere and is involuntarily represented by mankind." As that becomes visible to you, it changes your whole understanding of the functioning of the collective psyche of humanity—of the way it manifests itself, politically and religiously and factionally, in all of its various aspects.

8

Paragraphs 662-687 and the Book of Enoch

The basic theme of tonight's assignment is the differentiation and transformation of the God-image in history. And the data that Jung uses to demonstrate that differentiation and transformation are chiefly the vision of Ezekiel, the vision of Daniel and the vision in the Book of Enoch. The vision of Ezekiel comes from about the time of the Babylonian exile—so let's call it 550 B.C.; the Book of Enoch was completed about 100 B.C.; and the vision of Daniel falls somewhere in between.

The basic idea is that Job's encounter with Yahweh is followed by an activation of the collective unconscious by virtue of Job's profound conscious insight into the nature of the deity. The God-image feels obliged to move closer to man and that brings about the activation of the collective unconscious.

This tendency of the God-image to move closer to humankind is revealed first in Ezekiel's vision and then in a whole spate of apocalyptic literature that appears in the last two centuries B.C. Among the items of that literature Jung refers to are the Book of Daniel and the Book of Enoch. That's the basic theme of our subject matter. Having said that I now want to focus my remarks on eight items concerning this theme.

The first item is Ezekiel's vision which Jung discusses beginning in paragraph 665. The vision is of a great chariot with four massive wheels and above it is the vault of the heavens and sitting above that vault is the God-image "in the likeness of a human being." And each of the great wheels is surrounded by eyes all around its rims and each wheel is accompanied by a creature with four faces.

Jung speaks of this vision saying:

> The first great vision is made up of two well-ordered compound quaternities, that is, conceptions of totality, such as we frequently observe today as spontaneous phenomena. Their *quinta essentia* is represented by a figure which has "the likeness of a human form." Here Ezekiel has seen the essential content of the unconscious, namely

the idea of the higher man by whom Yahweh was morally defeated and who he was later to become.

This vision is really the culmination of the Old Testament, understood psychologically, and it's the foundation for Christian mandalas of Christ supported by the four evangelists, three of whom have animal faces and one of whom has a human face. It's the starting point for all later Jewish mysticism. Jung used this same image as the basic pattern for his formula of the Self which he describes in considerable detail in *Aion.*

This vision is found in chapter one of the Book of Ezekiel. Let me just read you a few of the passages to remind you of the flavor of this great vision of the God-image, the most differentiated depiction of the God-image in the Old Testament. You see, a process of differentiation has occurred as a result of the encounter with Job. The God-image is no longer so diffuse. It's undergone a *separatio* into four, so to speak.

> Storm wind from the north . . . huge cloud with flashing fire . . . four living creatures within the cloud. Each has four faces: one has the face of a man, one the face of a lion, one the face of an ox and one the face of an eagle. And there were wheels on the ground, one beside each of the four living creatures. Rims full of eyes all around. And over the heads of the living creatures something like a firmament could be seen like glittering crystal. And above the firmament something like a throne looking like sapphire and upon it was seated one that had the appearance of a man. [Here for the first time Yahweh is manifesting as a man which indicates that he's drawing closer to humanity. He's beginning to undergo humanization.] Fire is all about surrounded with splendor like the rainbow that appears in the clouds on a rainy day.[72]

And then in the next chapter Ezekiel hears a voice from the figure above. And the voice says,

> Son of man, stand up, I wish to speak with you. Son of man, I am sending you to the Israelites, rebels who have rebelled against me.[73]

---

[72] Ezek. 1:4-28, New American Bible (condensed).

[73] Ezek. 2:1-3, New American Bible (condensed).

So he addresses Ezekiel with the title, "Son of Man." In paragraph
667 Jung says that presumably that is meant to indicate that Ezekiel is
the son of the "Man" on the throne.

All right, that's the first piece of data Jung adduces to indicate that
the God-image is undergoing differentiation and transformation.

Jung's second reference and our second item is the vision of
Daniel which he speaks of in paragraph 668:

> The disturbance of the unconscious continued for several centuries.
> Around 165 B.C., Daniel had a vision of four beasts and the
> "Ancient of Days," to whom "with the clouds of heaven there came
> one like a son of man." Here the "son of man" is no longer the
> prophet but a son of the "Ancient of Days" in his own right, and a
> son whose task it is to rejuvenate the father.

This reference is found in the seventh chapter of Daniel, starting
with the second verse:

> In a vision I saw during the night suddenly the four winds of heaven
> stirring up the great sea from which emerged four immense beasts.
> One was like a lion, the second was like a bear . . . the third was
> like a leopard and the fourth, different from all the others, [was] terri-
> fying, horrible and of extraordinary strength . . . and had iron teeth.
> And as I watched . . . thrones were set up and the ancient one, the
> ancient of days took his throne. His clothing was snow bright and
> the hair on his head as white as wool. His throne was flames of fire
> with wheels of burning fire. . . . A surging stream of fire flowed out
> from where he sat. Thousands upon thousands were ministering to
> him and millions upon millions attended him. . . . As the vision
> continued I saw one like a Son of Man coming on clouds of heaven
> and when he reached the ancient of days and was presented before him
> he received dominion, glory and kingship. Nations and peoples of
> every language serve him. His dominion is an everlasting dominion
> that shall not be taken away. His kingship shall not be destroyed.[74]

So here again we have the God-image manifesting in a vision to
man and appearing first of all as an old man and then as someone
designated as the Son of Man who represents a rejuvenation of the
antiquated God-image of the Ancient of Days. And just as in

---

[74] Dan. 7:2-14, New American Bible (condensed).

Ezekiel's vision there is a quaternity of figures that are described as four animals, one of them of a different nature. It doesn't indicate what the nature is. Here we encounter that characteristic theme of the three plus one, the so-called Axiom of Maria.[75] So that's the second batch of data about the changing of the God-image.

The third batch, and our third item today, comes up in reference to the Book of Enoch. Now, I hope you've looked into it and have some idea of its content. It's diffuse, it's not well ordered and I think that's probably because it's a composite. It's likely a compilation of a number of visionary experiences—perhaps of more than one author. And it's written over a period of time, probably at least half a century.

Let me just outline the essential features of that portion of the book of Enoch that concerns us.

In chapters 7-16 we learn about the fallen angels who have been lured down because of the attractions of the daughters of men, and they descend from heaven and take wives and live human lives and teach humanity the arts and sciences. But also the children that they generate are giants who turn on humanity and begin to eat them. This is finally brought to God's attention and, as Jung points out, rather belatedly brought to his attention. He should have been aware of it immediately but he wasn't. And he then eventually punishes the fallen angels by binding them and casting them into darkness.

I'll just read you a bit out of the Book of Enoch to refresh your memories:

> Azazel taught man to make swords, knives, shields, breastplates, workmanship of bracelets and ornaments, the use of paint, the beautifying of the eyebrows, the use of stones, all sorts of dyes so that the world became altered. Impiety increased, fornication multiplied and they transgressed and corrupted all their ways. Another fallen angel taught sorcerers and dividers of roots . . . another the observations of the stars, another astronomy—the motion of the moon.[76]

---

[75] "One becomes two, two becomes three, and out of the third comes the One as the fourth." See Jung, *Psychology and Alchemy,* CW 12, par. 209.

[76] R.H. Charles, ed., *The Apocrypha and the Pseudepigrapha of the Old Testament in English,* vol. 2, p. 192 (condensed).

Then in chapters 17-37 Enoch takes a series of journeys through earth and hell, going in the four directions. This represents a characteristic *peregrinatio*. It's a circumambulation of the whole circumference of the world that involves again a quaternity because it is a visiting of each of the four directions in turn.

This is followed in chapters 39-43 by a journey to heaven. And there Enoch has a vision of the four sides of God. The sides representing three of the divine presences are busy praising God and one side is busy warding off the Satans that threaten to attack him.

In chapters 45-50 we have a vision of the Last Judgment, the image of the Ancient of Days, and the Son of Man who will pass judgment. There's a reference to that in chapter 46:

> I beheld the Ancient of Days whose head was like white wool [it's the same image as in Daniel] with whom was another whose countenance resembled that of man.
>
> And he was told this other was called the Son of Man. This is the "Son of Man to whom righteousness belongs, with whom righteousness has dwelt."

And as Jung notes, the great emphasis on righteousness is presumably connected with this because God had begun to realize that he was a bit deficient in that quality.

Then in chapter 59 we're told about Behemoth and Leviathan who will be served up as food for the faithful in the Last Judgment.

In chapter 70 Enoch beholds the crystal house of God and he is addressed by the God-image as the Son of Man:

> The Ancient of Days came and then that angel came to me and with his voice saluted me saying, "Thou art the Son of Man who art born for righteousness and righteousness hath rested on thee. The righteousness of the Ancient of Days shall not forsake thee."

So the Book of Enoch ends with the apotheosis of Enoch. He undergoes a deification because he is identified as the Son of Man which is a manifestation of the God-image. So much for the summary of the Book of Enoch.

I now want to pay special attention to some of the items of the summary. The first item concerns the giants, generated by the fallen angels, who start devouring mankind. I've reported a remarkable modern parallel to this account in Enoch—a dream that came to my attention. And I'll read you a portion of it. This is a dream of a man who later became a Jungian analyst:

> I am along what appears to be the Palisades, overlooking all of New York City. I am walking with a woman who is unknown to me personally, we are both being led by a man who is our guide. NYC is in a rubble—the world in fact has been destroyed. It's just one heap of rubble. There are fires everywhere, thousands of people are running in every direction frantically, the Hudson river has overflowed many areas of the city, smoke is billowing up everywhere. The land has been leveled. Fireballs were in the sky, heading for the earth. It was the end of the world.
>
> The cause of this great destruction was a race of great giants—giants who had come from outer space—from the far reaches of the universe. In the middle of the rubble I could see two of them sitting; they were casually scooping up people by the handful and eating them. The sight was awesome.[77]

The dream continues but this excerpt is enough to illustrate the modern evocation of the archetype of the end of the world which was first constellated in history in the context of Noah's flood. The archetype was constellated a second time in the context of the change of the aeons (at the beginning of our current aeon) which was Enoch's concern, and now the same image is showing up in the unconscious of individuals at the end of that aeon—in current times. It's a very vivid expression of the activation of the archetypal contents of the unconscious. That's what the giants represent—the archetypes. They're bigger-than-life things. And as they descend onto earth the image of their devouring human beings is an expression of individuals being eaten up by identification with the archetypes that are falling into the individual conscious psyche. So being devoured by giants is an image of succumbing to inflation.

The next item concerns that fourth side of the deity which is fending off "the Satans." Jung refers to that in paragraph 673 and 674:

> Enoch in his vision sees the four faces of God. Three of them are engaged in praising, praying, and supplicating, but the fourth in

---

[77] See also Edinger, *The Creation of Consciousness,* p. 28.

"fending off the Satans and forbidding them to come before the Lord of Spirits to accuse them who dwell on earth."

The vision shows us an essential differentiation of the God-image: God now has four faces.

In addition, Satan has now been excluded from the God-image and there's a conscious dynamic at work to keep him separate.

Jung says in paragraph 674 that one of these faces

is exclusively occupied in keeping his elder son Satan, now changed into many, away from him, and in preventing further experiments after the style of the Job episode.

An interesting almost modern parallel to this image is found at the beginning of Goethe's *Faust*. I can't say for sure but I very much doubt that Goethe was familiar with the Book of Enoch. Anyway, his "Prologue in Heaven" (the opening scene of *Faust)* starts out the same way as the Book of Job—with Mephistopheles visiting the court of heaven and putting his wager to the Lord. The prologue of *Faust* begins with the archangels Gabriel, Raphael and Michael, each in turn, singing the praises of Creation—how glorious is the Creation of the Lord. One, two, three—they come out and then along comes Mephistopheles and says, "I'm sorry I can't give your Creation any praise—it looks like a complete mess to me." That's number 4, you see—three plus one—it is the same image as the Book of Enoch, the difference being that there's nothing to fend Mephistopheles off. He just saunters into the heavenly court and starts expressing himself.

Now our next item, number 6, is referred to in paragraph 675. That the Satans were excluded in Enoch, Jung points out, indicates "a metaphysical split" has already taken place between Yahweh and Satan. Then Jung goes on to say:

But the pleromatic split is in its turn a symptom of a much deeper split in the divine will: the father wants to become the son, God wants to become man, the amoral wants to become exclusively good, the unconscious wants to become consciously responsible.

I think we've got four equations there that are worth detailed consideration.

1) "The split in the divine will," he says, means "the father wants

to become the son," meaning that an aging process is recognized that is calling for rejuvenation, rebirth.

2) "God wants to become man" means the eternal, the immutable, the archetypal and universal want to be humanized, they want to manifest in time, they want to incarnate, they want to have existence in particularity—in time and space—to submit to the limitation in order to manifest more concretely.

3) "The amoral wants to become exclusively good." The amoral refers to the unconscious state of the God-image which exists prior to moral differentiation—prior to the separation of the opposites. It wants to separate the opposites and then identify exclusively with the good which can take place only by becoming human. It can't occur as long as the God-image remains in an eternal undifferentiated form. It has to allow itself to go through human incarnation in order to achieve that differentiation.

4) "The unconscious wants to become consciously responsible." There again full consciousness of the Self requires a particular incarnated human ego in order to be the Self's vessel of realization.

All of those four equations refer to the process of the differentiation and transformation of the unconscious as it is encountered by the conscious ego. And all four equations describe the dynamics of what goes on when the unconscious is subjected to scrutiny—a serious examination, a serious *auseinandersetzung* and a serious attempt by the conscious ego to come to terms with it.

Item 7 is this term "Son of Man." It came up in the vision of Ezekiel, in the vision of Daniel and it comes up again in the Book of Enoch. This is a complex symbolic image of great dynamism. A whole book has been written on the symbolism of the Son of Man.[78] This image drew so much attention, of course, because Christ used this term repeatedly to refer to himself. The term Son of Man occurs eighty times in the four Gospels. But as I say, it didn't begin there. It began with Ezekiel, Daniel and Enoch—all of them long before Christ.

Religious scholars have disputed endlessly about this term and their interpretations fall into four categories:

---

[78] F.H. Borsch, *The Son of Man in Myth and History.*

1) *The personalistic-reductive category.* According to this view the term doesn't mean anything special at all. It just means "human being." It's the same as saying, "Man, it's cold outside."

2) *The archetypal interpretation.* According to this view, Son of Man refers to the original man, or Anthropos, that first appeared in early Near Eastern myth. So that a synonym for Son of Man according to the archetypal interpretation might be "primal Man" —Man spelled with a capital M.

3) This is what I call *the messianic category* which refers to a pre-ordained, special elect one—a figure who is to appear on earth and lead a life of suffering in order to redeem mankind. This is something akin to the "suffering servant" of Isaiah.

4) *The eschatological view.* According to this view the Son of Man is a metaphysical figure who is an aspect or partner of Yahweh, of God, who will manifest himself at the end of time, when he will pass judgment (the Last Judgment).

These are the kind of complex, multifaceted interpretations you get when you're dealing with a true symbol. When a true symbol is alive it won't stand still for a single interpretation.

Psychologically, I think we can get some idea of what the term Son of Man means by comparing it with a similar term used in alchemy. In alchemy one of the synonyms for the Philosopher's Stone is the *filius philosophorum,* the son of the philosophers. You see, that's very similar to the Son of Man. "Philosophers" is a name that the alchemists use for themselves. They were the philosophers. So the son of the philosophers is equivalent to the son of the alchemists. It's the son of the people who made it. And what that signifies is that they considered the stone to be a product of human effort—although with God's help.

I believe the term Son of Man has a similar psychological connotation. It's an image of the Self. It represents a rejuvenation of the God-image which is now appearing in a younger version—but not under the appellation Son of God (though that is sometimes used as an alternative). But in the context in which I have been talking about it, at any rate, it's called Son of Man, which signifies that the newborn transformed image of the Self represents a sum or product of human consciousness. In other words, the God-image in its con-

scious, transformed state emerges as the result of an encounter with a
conscious human ego. And that's why it's called Son of Man.

Now let's see what Jung says about this. He refers to it first in
paragraph 677:

> When Yahweh addressed Ezekiel as "Son of Man," this was no more
> at first than a dark and enigmatic hint. But now it becomes clear: the
> man Enoch is not only the recipient of divine revelation but is at the
> same time a participant in the divine drama, as though he were at
> least one of the sons of God himself. This can only be taken as
> meaning that in the same measure as God sets out to become man,
> man is immersed in the pleromatic process. He becomes, as it were,
> baptized in it and is made to participate in the divine quaternity (i.e.,
> is crucified with Christ).

You see that's quite an idea here, this idea that "man is immersed
in the pleromatic process." And Jung follows that up in paragraph
681, where he puts it this way:

> Enoch is addressed by the revealing angel with the title "Son of
> Man," a further indication that he, like Ezekiel, has been assimilated
> by the divine mystery, is included in it, as is already suggested by
> the bare fact that he witnesses it. . . . Enoch is wafted away and
> takes his seat in heaven . . . he beholds the house of God built of
> crystal. . . . The "Head of Days" comes forth and [says] "This is the
> Son of Man who is born into righteousness."

Here the striking phrase is that Enoch "has been assimilated by the
divine mystery, is included in it . . . by the bare fact that he wit-
nesses it."

You see, that's one of the features of the ego's encounter with the
unconscious. The very process of witnessing it drags one into it and
one becomes, willy-nilly, a participant in the process. The status of
remote observer is not possible in the process of encounter with the
unconscious. You can't see it as it really is unless you participate,
and then by the bare fact of witnessing the nature of the unconscious
you change it and you are drawn into the divine drama that it is an
expression of.

9

Paragraphs 688-712

Before we get into tonight's material, there is one item I wanted to finish up from last time. The reference comes from paragraph 686 where Jung says:

> The inner instability of Yahweh is the prime cause not only of the creation of the world, but also of the pleromatic drama for which mankind serves as a tragic chorus. The encounter with the creature changes the creator.

I want to focus on that remark, "The encounter with the creature changes the creator," in order to apply it to our actual psychological experience. We get two terms here: creator and creature. Creature means the one created by the creator. So a question that immediately comes up when you reflect on this statement is, "Does the ego actually experience itself as a creature created by a creator?" Is that an actual ego experience for modern men and women? The answer to that question determines one's religious position in relation to existence.

Basically there are three possible religious positions concerning these terms creature and creator. First is what I call credo containment. Second is secular, rationalistic alienation, usually accompanied by inflation. And third is ego/Self dialogue, or individuation.

1) *Credo containment* refers to a state of affairs in which the ego experiences itself as the creature, as the created one, of a creator God, who has revealed himself in a particular religious creed, in a particular body of scripture. The rules of that creed are then experienced as the will of God, and the creature ego then subordinates itself to the will of God as revealed in the creed disseminated by the priesthood or clergy of the creed.

2) *The secular, rationalistic condition,* which is basically atheistic. According to this mode of experience, there is no transpersonal agency that is relevant to human existence. So the ego does not experience itself as a creature created by a creator God. Rather it experiences itself as a random phenomenon, a product of chance, and no

92

values exist beyond what the ego creates for itself. This is the modern, secular rationalistic/existentialist position.

3) *Ego/Self dialogue or individuation.* In this state of affairs the ego does indeed experience itself as the creature of a creator Self— one that must be given constant attention and connection but must also not be confined to any single creed. It is rather individual, personal experience that leads to the awareness that the ego is the creature of a transpersonal creator. It is only in this third mode of being that Jung's statement applies, "The encounter with the creature changes the creator." It is only in this third mode that any real encounter takes place between the creature and the creator, because only out of this religious position can a genuine *dialogue* occur.

As an illustration we can see two of these positions at work in the conflict over the teaching of evolution in the public schools. The credo containment attitude takes the position that a creator did indeed generate human life. But that conviction comes out of a particular religious creed. And of course the secular, rationalistic standpoint denies any transpersonal factor. The third possibility has not yet even entered the realm of public discussion. It doesn't exist, there is no spokesman for that third position at all.

I wanted to elaborate on that particular statement a bit because I think it orients us to keep in mind these three modes of religious stance whenever we encounter a new patient starting analysis. We ask ourselves, "Where is this person? Is the person coming from a position of credo containment or a secular, rationalistic position?" Those are the two positions we are most likely to encounter.

Now to tonight's material. The first item comes from paragraph 689:

> Jesus, it is plain, translated the existing tradition into his own personal reality, announcing the glad tidings: "God has good pleasure in mankind. He is a loving father and loves you as I love you, and has sent me as his son to ransom you from the old debt." He offers himself as an expiatory sacrifice that shall effect the reconciliation with God.

Jung goes on to remark how astonishing it is to discover that Yahweh's vindictiveness is so great that he must be bought off with the sacrifice of his son.

I want to talk a bit about this theme of Christ as an expiatory sacrifice. The image also comes up in the Book of Revelation where Christ appears in the image of a lamb who has been sacrificed. That's one of his synonyms, the sacrificial lamb. What we encounter here is a continuation, on another level, of the sacrificial ritual of the traditional Hebrew ceremonies. Animal sacrifice was a prominent feature of Israelite religion, and Christ took over that tradition. As Jung puts it, "Jesus translated the existing tradition into his own personal reality." The existing tradition was the sacrificial religion of animal sacrifice which Christ translated into his own reality.

That is illustrated with particular clarity in the Book of Hebrews. The following is a paraphrase from the ninth chapter:

> The first covenant had rules for worship and a man-made place for worship as well. A tabernacle tent is put up and after arrangements are made, the tabernacle erected, the outer holy place and the Inner Holy of Holies, the priests go into the outside tent every day to perform their duties, but only the High Priest goes into the inside tent, and he does this only once a year. He takes with him blood, the blood of the sacrificial animal which he offers to God on behalf of himself and for the sins of the people. And the Holy Spirit clearly teaches, from all these arrangements, that the way into the Most Holy Place has not yet been opened, as long as the outside tent still stands. This is a figure which refers to the present time. It means that the gifts and animal sacrifices offered to God cannot make the worshipper's heart perfect, they have to do only with food, drink and various cleansing ceremonies. These are outward rules only, which apply only until the time when God will reform all things.
>
> But Christ has already come as the High Priest and the tent in which he serves is greater and more perfect. It is a tent not made by human hands. And when Christ went through that tent and entered once and for all into the Most Holy Place, he did not take the blood of goats and calves, rather he took his own blood, and attained eternal salvation for us. The blood of goats and bulls and the ashes of the bull calf are sprinkled on the people who are ritually unclean, and that makes them clean. And since this is true, how much more is accomplished by the blood of Christ. He offers himself as a perfect sacrifice to God. His blood will make our consciences clean.[79]

---

[79] Heb. 9:1-14, Good News Bible (slightly modified).

So you see there is a precise transfer from the sacrificial ritual of the Hebrews to the self-sacrifice of Christ.

When you reflect on it, it is really quite astonishing how basic the archetype of sacrifice is to the human psyche. The majority of primitive societies have some vestiges of human sacrifice, and there is evidence in the Bible that the original sacrifice was a human sacrifice and only later did it become an animal sacrifice. The idea grips the primitive mind very profoundly that human existence requires a sacrifice to the divine agency, and these sacrifices can be terribly brutal affairs. The Aztecs give us a great example of that.

But what has happened now, according to the way Jung is laying it out, is that because of Yahweh's encounter with Job, Yahweh himself must now submit to sacrifice. Heretofore he has imposed on his creatures the sacrificial requirement. But now he must submit to it himself. Jung elaborates this whole idea in the Kotschnig letter that I referred to previously. He speaks of how Christ was

> up against an unpredictable and lawless God who would need a most drastic sacrifice to appease His wrath, viz. the slaughter of His own son. Curiously enough, as on the one hand his self-sacrifice means admission of the Father's amoral nature, he taught on the other hand a new image of God, namely that of a Loving Father in whom there is no darkness. . . . As a consequence the sacrifice was a self-destruction of the amoral God, incarnated in a mortal body. Thus the sacrifice takes on the aspect of a highly moral deed, of self-punishment as it were.[80]

To the extent that Christ is represented as the son of God, as Deity, then *his self-sacrifice is a self-destruction of the amoral God, who demands such human sacrifices.* To that extent, then, he is evidence of God's goodness. His role was to sacrifice himself in that fashion.

I would draw your attention to an important discussion of the psychology of sacrifice in Jung's essay, "Transformation Symbolism in the Mass."[81] The theme of sacrifice is very important in individuation imagery.

---

[80] *Letters,* vol. 2, p. 313.
[81] *Psychology and Religion,* CW 11, pars. 381ff.

The next item I want to talk about is paragraph 692.

The sending of the Paraclete has still another aspect. This Spirit of Truth and Wisdom is the Holy Ghost by whom Christ was begotten. He is the spirit of physical and spiritual procreation who from now on shall make his abode in creaturely man. Since he is the Third Person of the Deity, this is as much as to say that *God will be begotten in creaturely man.* This implies a tremendous change in man's status. . . . But that puts man, despite his continuing sinfulness, in the position of the mediator, the unifier of God and creature.

This reminds one of the symbolism of the Trinity, three unified and yet separate entities, Father, Son and Holy Ghost (or Holy Spirit; somehow I like Holy Ghost a little better, it has a little more shadow to it). According to the Western creed, the Son proceeds from the Father and the Holy Ghost proceeds from the Father and the Son. This differs from the Eastern Church where the Holy Ghost proceeds from the Father alone. This indicates the importance that the Western Church mythologically attaches to the ego.

The idea Jung is putting forward here is that the Holy Ghost is going to manifest itself not only in its original vessel, of Christ, but now also in sinful man. This is his idea of continuing incarnation. I want to draw your attention to an important discussion of the Holy Ghost that Jung gives us in a letter to Father Lachat, found in volume 18 of the *Collected Works* and reprinted in the paperback *Psychology and Western Religion.* Jung has a number of very pertinent things to say there about the nature of the Holy Ghost as it generates the continuing incarnation.

This gentleman, Father Lachat, had written a book on the Holy Ghost and, in Jung's view, missed the whole point—so much so that Jung was stirred to express himself:

Thus the ordinary man became a source of the Holy Spirit. . . . This fact signifies the continued and progressive divine incarnation. Thus man is received and integrated into the divine drama. He seems destined to play a decisive part in it; that is why he must receive the Holy Spirit. I look upon the receiving of the Holy Spirit as a highly revolutionary fact which cannot take place until the ambivalent nature of the Father is recognized. . . . A conscientious clarification of the idea of God would have consequences as upsetting as they are necessary. They would be indispensable for an interior development of the trinitarian drama and of the role of the Holy Spirit. The Spirit is destined to be incarnate in man or to choose him as a transitory dwelling-place.[82]

This is the symbolic description that Jung is using to describe the effects of an ego's having a serious engagement with the unconscious. When that occurs a continuing incarnation is taking place and humankind is received and integrated into the divine drama.

Continuing the discussion of the Holy Ghost, the next item comes from *Answer to Job,* paragraph 695:

> Although the Paraclete is of the greatest significance metaphysically, it was, from the point of view of the organization of the Church, most undesirable, because, as is authoritatively stated in scripture, the Holy Ghost is not subject to any control. In the interests of . . . the Church . . . the continuing indwelling of the Holy Ghost is discouraged and ignored as much as possible. No further individualistic digressions can be tolerated [i.e., that just leads to heresy].

And the way that was accomplished was that at Pentecost, when the Holy Ghost descended, it descended on Mary who was therefore understood to be the personification of the Church.[83] And so at Pentecost the Church was born. That's the birthday of the Church—Pentecost, it's the offspring of the Holy Ghost. That meant that henceforth the Holy Ghost was safely chained up in the Church. The Church then becomes the arbiter of the Holy Ghost. This illustrates how dangerous the Holy Ghost is for all group life. Every group organism attempts to chain up the Holy Ghost, and then the label of heresy is attached to any manifestation of the Holy Ghost that runs contrary to what the canon of the given group is.

The next item comes from paragraph 696:

> In Christ's sayings there are already indications of ideas which go beyond the traditionally "Christian" morality—for instance the parable of the unjust steward, the moral of which agrees with the Logion of the Codex Bezae.

---

[82] "Letter to Père Lachat," *The Symbolic Life,* CW 18, par. 1551.

[83] This is discussed in Edinger, *The Christian Archetype: A Jungian Commentary on the Life of Christ,* pp. 123-130.

That Logion or saying of Jesus is one that Jung refers to a number of times throughout his work, and he quotes it again in a footnote to the passage I just read:

> "Man, if indeed thou knowest what thou doest, thou are blessed; but if thou knowest not, thou art cursed, and a transgressor of the law."

That is the remark Christ made when he came across a man working on the Sabbath, and some Pharisees said to him, "How about that?" It was about as bad as murder, in ancient Israel, to work on the Sabbath. And yet according to this Logion, if you know what you are doing, you can get away with it; and if you don't, you are cursed. That's a truth I think we all recognize as profoundly applicable to a relation to the unconscious. When dubious things come up that are contrary to the conventional morality, if one acts in accordance with such things everything depends on the degree of consciousness with which those actions are taken.

The next item comes from paragraph 698 where Jung talks about John, the author of the Epistles of John, who declared that God is light and that "in him is no darkness at all."

> John is a bit too sure, and therefore he runs the risk of a dissociation. Under these circumstances a counterposition is bound to grow up in the unconscious, which can then irrupt into consciousness in the form of a revelation. If this happens, the revelation will take the form of a more or less subjective myth, because, among other things, it compensates the one-sidedness of an individual consciousness. This contrasts with the visions of Ezekiel or Enoch, whose conscious situation was mainly characterized by an ignorance (for which they were not to blame) and was therefore compensated by a more or less objective and universally valid configuration of archetypal material.

I wanted to draw your attention to that remark because it applies to our understanding of dreams. Just as there are two kinds of compensatory visions (such as the ones Jung mentions in the above passage), so there are two kinds of compensatory dreams. Jung tells us that practically all dreams are compensatory in one way or another. But they can be compensatory in different ways.

It is vitally important to understand the state of the dreamer's consciousness before trying to interpret a dream, because the compensatory element in the dream can be of two kinds:

1) If the consciousness of the dreamer is decidedly one-sided in certain respects, then the dream will have a marked tendency to compensate that one-sidedness by over-emphasizing the contrary, the opposite. One is most apt to find that situation among patients at the very beginning of analysis. Often they come in with one-sided conscious standpoints.

2) The other kind of compensation really isn't compensation, strictly speaking, at all. It is rather a situation in which the individual ego is ignorant and innocent of a whole layer of meaning, and in that case the dream brings up meanings that are objectively true and that compensate, so to speak, for the innocent ignorance but not in the usual sense of compensation. The dream, then, is more an objective description of the way things are. I think as analysis proceeds this is the more usual kind of dream though the more ordinary compensatory dreams (of the first type) will also appear occasionally, especially when the patient gets caught in a particularly one-sided conscious attitude.

For the rest of tonight and for next week's assignment we will be studying Jung's discussion of the Book of Revelation. Let me offer you an outline of this book:

Chapters 1-3. A vision of the Son of Man, with a two-edged sword coming out of his mouth, followed by the seven letters to the seven churches, somewhat threatening letters.

Chapters 4-11. A grand vision of the divine throne, of a crystalline deity, the four animals, the sacrificial lamb with the seven horns and seven eyes, which animal then opens the scroll with the seven seals. And these seven seals are broken, one by one. Each time a seal is broken a calamity descends upon the earth. The first four seals are the so-called "Four Horsemen of the Apocalypse," riding a white horse, a red horse, a black horse and a pale horse—a kind of apocalyptic quaternity. After the seven seals we have seven angels with seven trumpets, and as each one sounds her trumpet additional calamities pour down upon the earth.

Chapters 12-13. The vision of the sun-woman and the dragon, the woman clothed in the sun standing on the moon, who gives birth to a son who is caught up to heaven.

Chapters 14-16. The announcement of the eternal gospel which is "Fear God and give him glory." Then we have the vision of the wine-press of God's anger and the harvest which is the slaughter of humanity. Then more plagues pour out on humanity from the seven bowls.

Chapters 17-18. The Great Whore of Babylon, who is drunk with the blood of the saints.

Chapters 19-20. The final battles in which Satan is bound and cast into an abyss and into a lake of fire, with the Resurrection of the Dead and the Last Judgment.

Chapters 21-22. The grand image of the heavenly Jerusalem, the great mandala vision and the grand image of the Marriage of the Lamb to the heavenly Jerusalem.

That's the outline that I will flesh out for you in the next two meetings, but for now I want to speak of the Book of Revelation as a whole. You see it's a massive image of the activation of the collective unconscious, the coming of the Self and its conscious realization.

It is expressed largely in negative terms up until the very end. This book is the Western psyche's classic example of the archetype of the end of the world. Other terms for this same archetype would be "cosmic catastrophe" and "last judgment."[84] You see then how the extreme and destructive imagery associated with this image of the coming of the Self indicates that the ego in our current aeon experiences this event as a disaster.

If we put it in calm, objective, clinical terms, what this imagery is picturing is the process of the relativization of the ego. It sounds harmless enough, doesn't it? But to the ego when it is undergoing its own relativization it does not seem harmless. That is the event that occurs when the ego has a decisive encounter with the Self. That experience, almost regularly, is accompanied by terror and the sense of catastrophic destruction, because the ego is centered in itself, you see, and the prospect of being judged and relativized is an absolute disaster when one encounters it decisively. Another image for the ego's encounter with the Self is the theme of the Eye of God. That is

---

[84] See also chapters 8 and 10 for discussions of this archetype.

a variation of this apocalyptic imagery.[85]

This theme of cosmic catastrophe, or the end of the world, is a common delusion with the onset of psychosis. In such cases the death or relativization of the ego is equated with the death of the world, and rightly so, since the world exists only to the extent that there is a conscious ego to perceive it.

The end of the world theme also frequently appears in dreams. Nowadays the most common examples are dreams of nuclear war or nuclear explosions of one kind or another, which are images of eruption into conscious manifestation of the nucleus of the psyche, the Self. These dreams more often than not are highly positive, even though they strike terror in the individual. Whenever you encounter dreams of that sort, think of Revelation, because one of the important images is fire falling from heaven. It fits the imagery of nuclear war precisely.

---

[85] See *The Creation of Consciousness,* pp. 42ff.

10

Paragraphs 713-733

You remember last time, when we started looking at the Book of Revelation as a psychological document, I spoke of it as a massive symbolic image representing the activation of the collective unconscious and the eruption of awareness of the Self into consciousness. I mentioned that dreams of this archetype of the end of the world, the cosmic catastrophe, are not infrequent in modern experience. Dreams of nuclear war and nuclear explosions are the most common examples. I also mentioned that these dreams in their net effect are often not as negative or destructive as they may first appear.

I want to give you a particularly vivid example of such a dream. It is described in rather fulsome terms, and I'm just going to let the dream speak for itself. It was dreamt by a middle-aged woman who had been in analysis for several years. She labeled this dream, "The Paradise Bomb Shelter."

> We were in a room which was somewhere between being a bomb shelter and the fortified inner city of an ancient holy town, such as Acre or Jerusalem. The walls were foursquare and between the wall and the room or the building there was a corridor of air, something like an overgrown, encircling apartment house airshaft—a buffer region, a no-man's land. And in this room privileged company sat, crouching, waiting until we hear the terrible explosion of the bomb descending on the outer world. It happens, and the din and the shaking take over, then they recede.
>
> We have been told that so long as we stay inside the walls and so long as we don't open the huge bronze doors, everything within the shelter will remain free from radiation or fallout and there will be no death by contamination. A group of five of us, feeling our hermetically sealed room is itself fated, and being filled with curiosity to see the ruined outer world—we run to the doors anyway and proceed to pull them open. That is, four of them do. I lose my nerve at the end and fall back to watch from a distance while the others proceed. Finally, with difficulty and great creaking noise the great bronze doors open, and as they do so they let in light—burning, blinding,

bitter-tasting, acrid-smelling, deafening, suffocating white light—which is radiation.

It doesn't take the four long to decide they have seen all they need to, and soon they are trying to close the doors again, and that is when I step out of my corner and I stand in the middle of the corridor, waiting their return, and as soon as the first one returns I catch her and embrace her warmly. She looks at me, startled but moved, and says, "Don't you realize that now, through touching me, you, too, are contaminated?"

I nod my head, "Yes, I do know," but that was the point. I wanted to share in her contamination. I wanted to indicate love, sympathy, admiration and a desire to be akin to all the consequences of the new human condition. Then I ask her, "What did you see outside?" and she answers, "Only a lot of broken glass."

Next we go about preparing for the deaths we feel sure will result from the exposure at the gates. Initially two people did die, but after that there are no further deaths, and it is as though the death rate has slowed down to normal. It is incredible. We had expected a ceaseless parade of dying and agonized radiation-sickened citizens, but now it begins to look as if it will take a lifetime for us all to die.

Then I see a family group, sitting as though for a formal portrait and I realize we had even been given the power of reproduction and generation, so this life is like the other, only we are free from the bind of stagnation and immortality. Through growth and decay we can change, and bomb shelters can become holy cities.

Well, I'm not going to offer any interpretation of that dream. It pretty well speaks for itself, showing you how what first appears as destructive nuclear light turns out on close inspection (at least when it is approached with the right conscious attitude), to be rather an image of initiation into authentic human existence, which includes, of course, mortality.

I want to go on to talk in more detail about this rich and complex Book of Revelation. There are a great many specific detailed images that are relevant to our psychological work, and I want to draw your attention to some of them, at least. The first chapter starts out with a vision of the numinosum in a particular form. John says:

> And I turned to see the voice that spake with me. And being turned, I saw seven golden candlesticks; And in the midst of the seven candlesticks one like unto to the Son of man, clothed with a garment down

to the foot, and girt about the paps with a golden girdle. His head and his hairs were white like wool, as white as snow; and his eyes were as a flame of fire; and his feet like unto fine brass, as if they burned in a furnace; and his voice as the sound of many waters. And he had in his right hand seven stars: and out of his mouth went a sharp two-edged sword: and his countenance was as the sun shineth in his strength.[86]

And quite understandably John then adds:

When I saw him, I fell at his feet as dead.[87]

This is a particularly interesting image of the Self as an instrument of *separatio.* The two-edged sword, which is a symbol of the Logos, is reminiscent of Christ's statement, "I came to bring not peace, but a sword," that is, to separate family members from each other. This image belongs to the whole symbol system of *separatio,* which I discuss in *Anatomy of the Psyche.*[88] Albrecht Dürer has a great picture of this particular image (opposite).

I also have come across another image of the same nature, the Self as it appears in the condition of *separatio.* It appears in the series of pictures that go to make up a case history I have published.[89] One of the pictures in that series was of a boy holding on to a balloon which was carrying him up into the sky, and as he went heavenward he came into the vicinity of a great saw-blade sun. The sun was pictured as a revolving sawblade, with rough, sharp teeth.[90] It is the same image as the image of Christ with the two-edged sword coming out of his mouth. In both cases the Self is manifesting as a sharp-edged instrument that divides. It is the kind of instrument that is most apt to show up in psychological situations where the Logos, the separating, judging function of the psyche, is insufficiently conscious. It is most

---

[86] Rev. 1:12-16. (All refs. to Revelation are from the Authorized Version)

[87] Rev. 1:17.

[88] Chapter 7, pp. 183-210.

[89] *[The Living Psyche: A Jungian Analysis in Pictures.* The book reproduces the 104 paintings produced by the patient (an artist) in the course of his analysis. The paintings are accompanied by descriptions, associations, dreams and active imaginings of the patient together with an incisive commentary by the author.—Ed.]

[90] See *The Living Psyche,* p. 22.

Christ of the Apocalypse
(From W. Kurth, ed., *The Complete Woodcuts of Albrecht Dürer)*

apt to show up in psychologies that are kind of diffuse and not very sharply discriminated. All that missing discrimination is residing in the Self, and it expresses itself in this kind of threatening image.

Another interesting item shows up a few verses after the one just quoted. The voice then explains to John what is meant by the stars and the candlesticks referred to in verses 12-16:

> The seven stars are the angels of the seven churches: and the seven candlesticks which thou sawest are the seven churches.[91]

So we have an image of seven candlesticks or lamps in the heavenly realm which are duplicated on the earthly realm as the seven churches. It is as though the seven archetypal luminosities are being mirrored on earth by the seven churches. Furthermore the seven stars are described as the "angels of the seven churches." And you will notice in the first verse of the next chapter that the letters written to each of the seven churches are addressed not to the church itself but to the angel of the church, so that the first letter reads, "Unto the angel of the Church of Ephesus, write . . . etc."

I think this image refers to a very interesting piece of psychological phenomenology that remains to be examined and elaborated, because I consider these angels of the churches to refer to the collective psychic organisms that the churches are examples of. There is only one other place in the Bible where this same image comes up—in the tenth chapter of Daniel. There an angel, in talking to Daniel, refers to an "angel of Persia, and an angel of Greece," and also mentions the fact that the archangel Michael is the guardian angel of Israel. So we are there told that nations have their angels as well as churches.

What I think those images refer to is the fact that every collective entity that is constituted by a group of individuals who are more or less identified with one particular collective theme, that every such collective entity is a separate psychic organism—it has an angel, so to speak. It transcends the mere existence of the individuals that compose it. It is as though the individuals form the cells of that larger organism. If you have such an idea, and start applying it to the way collective organisms behave, it can be very illuminating.

The next item is the so-called throne vision, found in the fourth

---

[91] Rev. 1:20.

chapter of Revelation:

> I was in the spirit: and, behold, a throne was set in heaven, and one
> sat on the throne. And he that sat was to look upon like a jasper and
> a sardine stone: and there was a rainbow round about the throne, in
> sight like unto an emerald. And round about the throne were four and
> twenty seats: and upon the seats I saw four and twenty elders sitting,
> clothed in white raiment; and they had on their heads crowns of gold.
> And out of the throne proceeded lightnings and thunderings and
> voices: and there were seven lamps of fire burning before the throne,
> which are the seven Spirits of God. And before the throne there was
> a sea of glass like unto crystal . . . and round about the throne, were
> four beasts full of eyes before and behind. And the first beast was
> like a lion, and the second beast like a calf, and the third beast had a
> face as a man, and the fourth beast was like a flying eagle.[92]

This throne symbolism, which occurred first of all in Ezekiel's
vision, and here again in John's, is an example of the archetype of
the chair. You might not think of a chair as an archetype, but it is.
The great cathedrals of Europe are magnificent buildings built around
a chair. *Cathedra* means chair, the chair that the bishop sits in. That
is why, when one addresses the "chair," one is addressing the head
of the organization—"Mr. Chairman." One is addressing the archetype. This shows up in dreams sometimes. Esther Harding wrote
about the symbolism of the analyst's chair.[93] She brought in a lot of
dreams as examples of how the chair of the analyst takes on archetypal authority and expresses itself. It becomes a kind of *cathedra,* and
analysts, you know, have a great tendency to speak *ex cathedra.*

The discussion of throne symbolism is followed, in the next few
chapters of Revelation, by a whole series of events. There is a scroll
with seven seals on it, each of which is opened, one at a time; and
then seven angels appear, and each one blows a trumpet. We've already had seven stars in the hand of the Son of Man, and the seven
lampstands, so that the archetype of seven is very prominent in this
material. And the question, of course, is "What does it mean?" The
only way that we can elaborate this kind of material with any kind of
empirical validity is by the method of amplification. We look around

---

[92] Rev. 4:2-7.
[93] See M. Esther Harding, *The Parental Image,* p. 226.

to see in what other context the number seven is to be found.

A prominent context in ancient thinking was the seven planetary spheres—the idea of the planetary ladder. According to this idea, as you ascend step by step from earth all the way up to the uppermost region, the area of the fixed stars, you pass through each of the seven planets and planetary spheres, and each of them represents a rung on the ladder. Then when you reach the eighth level you have achieved the very top, the level of the fixed stars. There are seven steps between earth and heaven, and that's why the number seven is associated with the initiation process. If you go through all seven grades then you are initiated into the very highest level. And seven is to eight as three is to four: it is on the way to totality. Seven is the last station before final totality on the second level so to speak. So that would be some of the implications then, of the number seven.

Another item I want to allude to is the question of the "marked one." In chapter seven we read:

> And I saw another angel ascending from the east, having the seal of the living God: and he cried with a loud voice to the four angels, to whom it was given [the power] to hurt the earth and the sea, Saying, Hurt not the earth, neither the sea, nor the trees, till we have sealed the servants of our God in their foreheads. And I heard the number of them which were sealed: and there were sealed an hundred and forty and four thousand of all the tribes of the children of Israel.[94]

In many of the medieval pictures of the Apocalypse there are illustrations of this process, and there are long lines of people waiting to get their seal, and each one comes up to get a seal on his forehead. Usually it is represented as a cross, an equilateral cross. Another version of the "marked ones" is in chapter fourteen:

> [These people] shall drink of the wine of the wrath of God. . . . And the smoke of their torment ascendeth up for ever and ever: and they have no rest day nor night, who worship the beast and his image, and whosoever receiveth the mark of his name.[95]

So here's another version. Those who have worshipped the beast have the mark of the beast on their forehead. They are marked for

---

94 Rev. 7:2-4.
95 Rev. 14:10-11.

damnation, just as the others are marked for salvation. This represents two versions of the same archetype, one positive and one negative. To be marked means to be set apart, to be one of the elect. All archetypes are bipolar and this one is too. You can be elected to be blessed or elected to be damned. But psychologically considered, when this image comes up in dreams we understand that as being marked for individuation. In the psychological context, it isn't an either/or; it is rather like that motto placed over the *coniunctio* castle in the *Chymical Wedding of Christian Rosencreutz*, for all who enter to see, "Congratulations and condolences."[96]

To be marked has a double implication and if you don't split the opposites it means you are going to get a share of both curses and blessings. This comes up in dreams not infrequently and it is easy to miss unless you know the archetype. All archetypes are missed, unless you know them. Unless you can recognize them they will just slip right by you. If you know them, then you can nail it down.

The next item is the theme of stars falling from heaven, found in Revelation 6:12:

> And I beheld, when he had opened the sixth seal, and, lo, there was a great earthquake; and the sun became black as sackcloth of hair, and the moon became as blood; and the stars of heaven fell unto the earth, even as a fig tree casteth her untimely figs, when she is shaken of a mighty wind.

And then again in Revelation 8:10:

> The third angel sounded, and there fell a great star from heaven, burning as [if] it were a lamp.

This belongs to the same symbolism as Satan's falling from heaven, or the angels that descended to marry the daughters of men in Genesis. It is the same image of descent, of archetypal material falling out of the transpersonal realm and into the ego. So it belongs to the same imagery of *coagulatio*. I give a dream example of this motif on page 90 of *Anatomy of the Psyche*. In this dream a piece of the moon fell out of the sky into a patient's apartment. That presaged

---

[96] Christian Rosencreutz (pseud. of Johann Valentin Andreae), *The Hermetick Romance, or the Chymical Wedding*, p. 30. (Cited by Jung in *Mysterium Coniunctionis*, CW 14, par. 37)

the assimilation of a bit of femininity that had previously been lacking in her ego.

Another item is the symbolism of "one third." In Revelation 8:7 we read:

> The first angel sounded, and there followed hail and fire mingled with blood, and they were cast upon the earth: and a third part of trees was burnt up, and all green grass was burnt up. And the second angel sounded, and as it were a great mountain burning with fire was cast into the sea: and the third part of the sea became blood; And the third part of the creatures which were in the sea, and had life, died; and the third part of the ships were destroyed. And the third angel sounded, and there fell a great star from heaven . . . and it fell upon a third part of the rivers. . . . and the third part of the waters became wormwood. . . . and the third part of the sun was smitten, and the third part of the moon, and the third part of the stars . . . was darkened.

On and on the theme of one third is repeated. We are forced to ask ourselves, "What does that mean?" It was a theme that came to my attention as a result of a very sizable dream I had some years ago. One of the images was that terrorists burst into a church service and slaughtered one third of the congregation. For some time I didn't get this dream, especially what that particular image was about. And then when I made the connection with the Book of Revelation, everything in the dream fell into place. Then I recognized the whole dream to be a Last Judgment dream, to be the equivalent to Revelation. As soon as I realized that it all became clear.

That's what happens when one finds the right amplification to a particular dream image. If you find the right amplification, it's illuminating. Suddenly a light is turned on and then you've got your bearings and you know what it is about. As soon as I realized that the significant amplification to that particular image was the Book of Revelation where all these one thirds are destroyed, I could see that my dream was an expression of the Apocalypse.

That still doesn't explain what the meaning of one third is. I gave some thought to that and my thoughts are expressed in a chapter in *Ego and Archetype* called "Trinity and Quaternity." It is my conclusion that the number three is not always just an amputated quaternity, which in some cases it is. But that, especially in terms of the psychology of younger persons, the number three is the number of ego-hood because it is the conscious ego that must function in time and space, and time and space are ordered around the number three. Eternity is ordered around the number four.

So I understand all this emphasis on one third being destroyed to indicate an assault on the number three. In other words, an assault on the ego attitude. This contrasts with the situation earlier in life when the original state of wholeness, which is a kind of latent fourness, must be assaulted by the number three. You will sometimes encounter dreams that illustrate that point.

One good example I recall is the dream of a young man, a *puer aeternus* type, who needed more "threeness" in his life. He dreamt that a pie was being divided up into triangular sections. The original wholeness was being assaulted by the triangle, you see, in order for the ego to come into fuller manifestation.

The next item is the "sun and moon" woman from chapter twelve of Revelation.

> And there appeared a great wonder in heaven; a woman clothed with the sun, and the moon under her feet, and upon her head a crown of twelve stars: And she being with child cried, travailing in birth, and pained to be delivered. And then there appeared another wonder in heaven; and behold a great red dragon, having seven heads and ten horns. . . . And his tail drew the third part of the stars of heaven, and did cast them to the earth: and the dragon stood before the woman . . . to devour her child as soon as it was born. And she brought forth a man child, who was to rule all nations with a rod of iron: and her child was caught up unto God, and to his throne. And the woman fled into the wilderness, where she hath a place prepared of God.[97]

Jung talks about this image which is quite important to him. He first refers to it in *Answer to Job*, paragraphs 710-711:

> There appeared in heaven, after the destruction of Jerusalem, a vision of the *sun-woman*. . . . She was in the pangs of birth, and before her stood a great red dragon that wanted to devour her child.
> This vision is altogether out of context. Whereas with the previous visions one has the impression that they were afterwards revised,

---

[97] Rev. 12:1-6.

rearranged, and embellished, one feels that this image is original and not intended for any educational purpose.

And in paragraph 713 Jung says :

The manchild is "caught up" to God, who is manifestly his father, and the mother is hidden in the wilderness. This would seem to indicate that the child-figure will remain latent for an indefinite time and that its activity is reserved for the future.

And then again, in paragraph 716:

Under those conditions the new-born man-child would have been bound to have a noticeably positive aspect, because, in accordance with his symbolic nature, he would have compensated the intolerable devastation wrought by the outburst of long pent-up passions, being the child of the conjunction of opposites, of the sunfilled day world and the moonlit night world. He would have acted as a mediator . . . and would thus have become a beneficent saviour who restored the balance.

Let me just state it baldly and not beat around the bush: I think we can consider this child of the sun-moon woman (who is the personification of the Sol-Luna *coniunctio)* as an anticipation of Jungian psychology, lodged right in the middle of the ancient text. You see, John's God-image was split because, as characteristic of that numinosum (for instance, the sword coming out of its mouth), *separatio* has been the key theme of the Christian aeon. And the man-child born of this sun-moon woman is a product of the *coniunctio,* rather than the *separatio,* and so it represents the unified God-image that only becomes possible in the Jungian aeon, and that will come about progressively with the continuing incarnation of the God-image in earthly man. That's how I understand what Jung is telling us when he says, in paragraph 713:

The man-child is "caught up" to God, who is manifestly his father, and the mother is hidden in the wilderness. This would seem to indicate that the child-figure will remain latent for an indefinite time and that its activity is reserved for the future.

The future is now, and Jung, who has understood and interpreted that image, is performing the function of bringing its meaning and its realization to fulfillment.

11
Paragraphs 734-747

I want to discuss a few items left over from last time. First is the eternal gospel which states, "Fear God and give glory to him."

And I saw another angel fly in the midst of heaven, having the everlasting gospel to preach unto them that dwell on the earth, and to every nation, and kindred, and tongue, and people, Saying with a loud voice, Fear God and give glory to him.[98]

This is an important feature of Revelation for Jung. He speaks of it in several places, one of them paragraph 733:

Could anyone in his right senses deny that John correctly foresaw at least some of the possible dangers which threaten our world in the final phase of the Christian aeon? He knew, also, that the fire in which the devil is tormented burns in the divine pleroma for ever. God has a terrible double aspect: a sea of grace is met by a seething lake of fire, and the light of love glows with a fierce dark heat of which it is said "ardet non lucet"—it burns but gives no light. That is the eternal, as distinct from the temporal, gospel: *one can love God but must fear him.*

Jung is here enunciating a very basic principle of his thought. The statement just quoted replaces the naive assumption that God is a conscious and all-loving being. The eternal gospel means that it refers to beyond time—the eternal gospel as opposed to the temporal gospel. A corollary to the principle that one can love God under certain favorable circumstances, but must fear him, is that anxiety is an expression of proximity to God. This is a very helpful orienting principle, because once you grasp its reality you have immediately shifted the level at which you are understanding your experience from the personal to the transpersonal. Once you really get it, that anxiety is a manifestation of proximity to God, then any other more personal explanations of the experience, while retaining some valid-

---

[98] Rev. 14:6-7.

ity of course, will be swallowed up by the deeper meaning.

The other thing Jung says here is that God's terrible double aspect is composed of a sea of grace which is met by a seething lake of fire. I find it helpful to represent that formulation in the abbreviated form I've indicated on the blackboard:

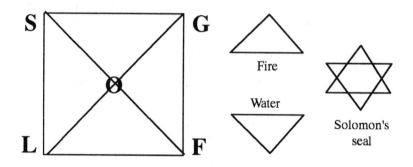

SOG signifies "sea of grace," LOF signifies "lake of fire"—they are all oriented around the central O, and when you represent it that way you have two triangles pointing in opposite directions. You've got the "sea of grace" triangle pointing downward, and the "lake of fire" triangle pointing upward. That corresponds to the alchemical emblems that I've indicated on the side—the downward pointing triangle in alchemy signifies water, and an upward pointing triangle signifies fire; and when you combine the two in the paradoxical union of fire and water you get that so-called Solomon's seal, or Star of David.

That's what we have here when we combine the sea of grace with the lake of fire. Jung is referring to this as the God-image, the nature of the God-image.

If any of you have any doubts about how closely you live right on the brink of the lake of fire, you can demonstrate it to yourself in only a few seconds. Just exhale and continue to do so until you can't stand it anymore, and you will immediately be plunged into the lake of fire. That's all it takes—it's right there in your physiology.

The next item is the Whore of Babylon:

And there came one of the seven angels which had the seven vials, and talked with me, saying unto me, Come hither, I will shew unto thee the judgment of the great whore that sitteth upon many waters: with whom the kings of the earth have committed fornication, and the inhabitants of the earth have been made drunk with the wine of her fornication. So he carried me away in the spirit into the wilderness: and I saw a woman sit upon a scarlet-coloured beast, full of names of blasphemy, having seven heads and ten horns. And the woman was arrayed in purple and scarlet colour, and decked with gold and precious stones and pearls, having a golden cup in her hand full of abominations and filthiness of her fornication: And upon her forehead was a name written, MYSTERY, BABYLON THE GREAT, THE MOTHER OF HARLOTS AND ABOMINATIONS OF THE EARTH. And I saw the woman drunken with the blood of the saints, and with the blood of the martyrs of Jesus.[99]

Jung says in paragraph 721 that this Great Whore of Babylon is "the counterpart of the heavenly Jerusalem." The heavenly Jerusalem is the great city mandala figure that we encounter at the very end of Revelation. The Great Whore of Babylon, continues Jung, is

the chthonic equivalent of the sun-woman Sophia, with, however, a reversal in moral character. If the elect turn themselves into "virgins" in honour of the Great Mother Sophia, a gruesome fantasy of fornication is spawned in the unconscious by way of compensation.

What we have here is the negative version of the personification of the city archetype. The heavenly Jerusalem is the positive version of the city archetype, and the Whore of Babylon is the negative version. It brings up the whole rich symbolism of the city. The city is the symbolic image of the feminine aspect of the Self. Babylon is its chthonic dark secular version, as contrasted with Jerusalem which is the heavenly, spiritual, divine version.

Aristotle said that man is a political animal. He wasn't referring to politics as we usually think of it, he was referring to the fact that man lives in a *polis*, a city, and that it is characteristic of the human condition to live in the city. That is why the very word "civilization" has as its root the word that means "city." The city is the mother of its inhabitants. The metropolis means, literally, the "mother city," so that when you read the "Metro" section of the *Los Angeles Times* you are

---

99 Rev. 17:1-6.

reading about the city archetype in its local manifestation.

In the Hebrew scriptures the two great symbolic cities are Babylon and Jerusalem. Jerusalem was the holy, sacred city, and Babylon was the despicable, secular city, because it was the city of captivity. It was the city of vice and luxury. It was the city that was hated by the Jews. It is all spelled out in Psalm 137, a captivity psalm:

> By the rivers of Babylon, there we sat down, yea, we wept, when we remembered Zion [Zion means Jerusalem]. We hanged our harps upon the willows in the midst thereof. For there they had carried us away captive required of us a song; and they that wasted us required of us mirth, saying, Sing us one of the songs of Zion. How shall we sing the Lord's song in a strange land? If I forget thee, O Jerusalem, let my right hand forget her cunning. . . . Rase it, rase it, even to the foundation thereof. O Daughter of Babylon, who art to be destroyed; happy shall he be that rewardeth thee as thou hast served us. Happy shall he be, that taketh and dasheth thy little ones against the stones.[100]

Babylon, from this period on, is the despicable city to be destroyed, and in Revelation that same symbolism was applied to Rome, which was the city that contained the whole civilized world at that time. John correctly predicted the fall of Rome, although it happened several centuries after he expected it. Augustine wrote a massive essay on the archetype of the city, called "City of God," where his basic idea is that history is divided by two cities formed by two alternative loves: the earthly city, created by creatures' love of themselves, and the heavenly city created by the love of God. One group wants to live after the flesh, and the other after the spirit; and Augustine specifically cites the heavenly Jerusalem as an example of the city of God, and Babylon as an example of the earthly city. Psychologically we would understand the earthly city to refer to the ego, and the heavenly city to the Self.

It is very interesting that in spite of the fact that the emerging split Christian mentality identified with the spirit and profoundly denigrated the earthly city, the Whore of Babylon was nevertheless represented as holding the golden cup, the image of supreme value. You

---

[100] Authorized Version.

may remember from our seminar on *Mysterium Coniunctionis* that this same image comes up in Ripley's *Cantilena,* where the pregnant queen drinks the blood of the green lion out of the golden cup of Babylon. Alchemy has here assimilated the golden cup of Babylon, plucked it right out of Revelation and put it into an alchemical context. The golden cup in the hands of the Whore indicates that she is carrying the symbolism of the Self despite the author's obvious intention to denigrate her.

In chapters nineteen and twenty of Revelation we read about a final battle, and then a Resurrection of the Dead, and the Last Judgment being meted out, and a reference to the Book of Life. This idea of resurrection would suggest that all repressed contents of the collective psyche are to be brought into view and accounted for. It is the idea that sooner or later the individual has to take responsibility for all repressed contents. You do not get away with anything, in the long run. I think all our psychological data verify that fact. In the short run, yes, but in the long run, no. There is a book of life that people are measured by. We find that in chapter twenty:

> And I saw the dead, small and great, stand before God [these are the dead that have been resurrected]; and the books were opened; and another book was opened, which is the book of life: and the dead were judged out of those things which were written in the books, according to their works. . . . And whosoever was not found written in the book of life was cast into the lake of fire.[101]

This same image comes up in a slightly different context in the tenth chapter of Luke, where Christ says to his disciples:

> Rejoice not, that the spirits are subject unto you; but rather rejoice, because your names are written in heaven.[102]

That's another reference to having your name written in the book of life. This image of the "big book" comes up in dreams every now and then, and when you come across it you can think of this particular passage in Revelation. I understand the image as picturing one's definitive relation to the Self.

---

[101] Rev. 20:12-15.
[102] Luke 10:20, Authorized Version.

So far as we can perceive, so far as our experience goes, there is no automatic guarantee at all that if one lives a life in continual violation of the realities of the Self one will eventually be forgiven. There isn't any evidence of that at all. The whole question of "Are there indeed damned souls?" can be put psychologically: "Is it possible to be permanently banished by the Self because of an ego life so egregiously in violation of the Self that it has become unredeemable?" We cannot answer that question in any final sense, but it is my impression that indeed there are such things as damned souls.

At the end of the Book of Revelation we are presented with the grand image of the heavenly Jerusalem descending from heaven, starting with the twenty-first chapter, verse 10:

> And he carried me away in the spirit to a great and high mountain, and shewed me that great city, the holy Jerusalem, descending out of heaven from God, And her light was like . . . a jasper stone, clear as crystal. The wall had twelve gates. On the east three gates, on the north three gates, on the south three gates, on the west three gates [it is a great mandala image]. And it was foursquare, 12,000 furlongs in each direction. And it was made of jasper and pure gold, all manner of precious stones, sapphire, calcedon, emerald, sardonyx, etc. And twelve gates were twelve pearls [where we get the idea of the "pearly gates to heaven]. The streets of the city were pure gold. And there was no temple there, for the Lord God Almighty . . . [is] the temple of it.[103]

And then starting with the twenty-second chapter:

> A pure river of the water of life proceeded out of the throne of God, and flowed through the city. The tree of life was blooming on it.[104]

Then Revelation goes on to speak of the marriage of the Lamb with the heavenly Jerusalem.

After describing the descent of the heavenly Jerusalem in just this way, Jung goes on to compare it with the vision of Ezekiel and in paragraph 727 refers to

> a fourfold synthesis of unconscious luminosities . . . of which the description of the heavenly city reminds us: everything sparkles with

---

[103] Rev. 21:10-22 (condensed and slightly modified).
[104] Rev. 22:1,2 (condensed and modified).

precious gems, crystal, and glass, in complete accordance with Ezekiel's vision of God. And just as the *hieros gamos* unites Yahweh with Sophia . . . thus restoring the original pleromatic state, so the parallel description of God and city points to their common nature: they are originally one, a single hermaphroditic being, an archetype of the greatest universality.

So what we have here then is the final *coniunctio* image in which the Heavenly City is married to the Sacred Lamb. That is the final *coniunctio,* and that particular imagery then shows up in Jung's grand *coniunctio* vision which he describes in *Memories, Dreams, Reflections.*[105]

The next item is a remark Jung makes in paragraph 716 in which he articulates an important operative principle:

> As a totality, the self is by definition always a *complexio oppositorum,* and the more consciousness insists on its own luminous nature and lays claim to moral authority, the more the self will appear as something dark and menacing.

In the Book of Revelation the Self appears as something profoundly dark and menacing, and we get small versions of this scenario in dreams all the time—threatening dreams. I think we can say that threatening dreams regularly have at least a faint reference to Revelation imagery. In analyzing such a dream the first thing that one has to determine is the nature of the conscious attitude that is constellating a dark and menacing response from the unconscious. Jung offers us guidance here, saying:

> The more consciousness insists on its own luminous nature and lays claim to moral authority [i.e., the more it is convinced of its rightness], the more the self will appear as something dark and menacing.

Another item: You will have noticed that Jung gives John a double interpretation. First, in paragraph 708, talking about the Book of Revelation he writes:

> We no longer recognize the meek Lamb who lets himself be led unresistingly to the slaughter; there is only the aggressive and irascible ram whose rage can at last be vented. In all this I see less a meta-

---

[105] See above, p. 64.

physical mystery than the outburst of long pent-up negative feelings such as can frequently be observed in people who strive for perfection.

Here Jung is giving us a personalistic interpretation of the rageful state of affairs in the Book of Revelation. But then we turn to paragraph 717 and he has changed his tune:

> But John's problem was not a personal one. It was not a question of his personal unconscious or of an outburst of ill humour, but of visions which came up from a far greater and more comprehensive depth, namely from the collective unconscious. His problem expresses itself far too much in collective and archetypal forms for us to reduce it to a merely personal situation. To do so would be altogether too easy as well as being wrong in theory and practice. . . . The eye of John penetrates into the distant future of the Christian aeon and into the dark abyss of those forces which his Christianity kept in equilibrium. What burst upon him is the storm of the times, the premonition of a tremendous enantiodromia.

How are we to understand this apparent reversal? This isn't the only occasion on which Jung can be accused of being inconsistent. You can almost say he is consistently inconsistent, and that is because he is always keenly aware of the operation of the opposites. Both the personal and the archetypal are appropriate, and which one is to be emphasized in a given situation often depends on clinical judgment. But certainly whenever one has dream material that has clear collective imagery (as in the Book of Revelation), we are informed immediately that the issue is more than a personal one. That doesn't mean it is not personal at all, it just means it is more than a personal issue.

But in order for anyone to tune in to an archetypal or collective issue, one has to have at least a smattering of the same material in his personal psychology in order to open the gate. That is usually easy enough since we are individually members of the collective psychic circumstance that surrounds us, therefore its issues are also going to penetrate us personally to a greater or lesser extent. But the point is that both of Jung's interpretations of John, the personal and the collective, are right. And in studying this material we can see just how Jung might proceed with a dream interpretation. He'd start out examining the personal dimension of the symbolism, and then, perceiving that the imagery was not adequately explained on that level, he would go on to the archetypal interpretation.

Paragraph 738:

> The paradoxical nature of God has a like effect on man: it tears him asunder into opposites and delivers him over to a seemingly insoluble conflict. What happens in such a condition? . . . There are, for example, conflicts of duty no one knows how to solve. Consciousness only knows: *tertium non datur!* [A third is not given.] The doctor therefore advises his patient to wait and see whether the unconscious will not produce a dream which proposes an irrational and therefore unexpected third thing as a solution. As experience shows, symbols of a reconciling and unitive nature do in fact turn up in dreams . . . signifying the union of opposites.

As I said earlier, the symptom of anxiety is a manifestation of proximity to God. Jung is now adding to that proposition another: that a state of conflict is a symptom of proximity to God. Conflict means that one is in the vicinity of the paradoxical God nature, and that proximity has the effect of tearing one asunder into opposites. When that happens the prescription is to wait—endure and wait—for the third.

The same issue is continued in paragraph 739:

> The opposition between God and man in the Christian view may well be a Yahwistic legacy from olden times, when the metaphysical problem consisted solely in Yahweh's relations with his people. The fear of Yahweh was still too great for anybody to dare—despite Job's gnosis—to lodge the antinomy in Deity itself. But if you keep the opposition between God and man, then you finally arrive, whether you like it or not, at the Christian conclusion, "omne bonum a Deo, omne malum ab homine" [all good from God, all bad from man], with the absurd result that the creature is placed in opposition to its creator and a positively cosmic or daemonic grandeur in evil is imputed to man.

Here's another very important Jungian principle, that the opposites reside in the God-image. That means good and evil, as well as the other opposites, are attributes of the God-image itself. If the ego falls into an identification with either one of a pair of opposites, it is then on its way to the absurd result that Jung alludes to. It is easy enough to state this principle, but it is not so easy to integrate and apply in actual psychological life, because the early development of the ego is based on taking responsibility for everything that goes on in the psyche. So it requires a revolutionary change in attitude to posit the opposites as residing in the God-image rather than in the ego.

Paragraph 740 contains a very important statement, a wonderful statement:

> Yahweh's decision to become man is a symbol of the development that had to supervene when man becomes conscious of the sort of God-image he is confronted with. God acts out of the unconscious of man and forces him to harmonize and unite the opposing influences to which his mind is exposed from the unconscious. The unconscious wants both: to divide and to unite. In his striving for unity, therefore, man may always count on the help of a metaphysical advocate, as Job clearly recognized. The unconscious wants to flow into consciousness in order to reach the light, but at the same time it continually thwarts itself, because it would rather remain unconscious. [Because it is composed of opposites, that is why it does these contradictory things.] That is to say, God wants to become man, but not quite.

And from paragraph 746:

> The only thing that really matters now is whether man can climb up to a higher moral level, to a higher plane of consciousness, in order to be equal to the superhuman powers which the fallen angels have [passed] into his hands.[106]

And then finally, at the end of paragraph 747, there is this pregnant statement:

> Since he has been granted an almost godlike power, he can no longer remain blind and unconscious. He must know something of God's nature and of metaphysical processes if he is to understand himself and thereby achieve gnosis of the Divine.

In practical terms I take this to mean that whenever we are pre-

---

[106] The text has "played," but I think "passed" is a better translation—the fallen angels have handed them over.

sented with archetypal dreams it is nearly always our obligation to bring in the so-called metaphysical dimension of the individual's existence, because the dreams are asking for that level to be included. Archetypal dreams are examples of the fallen angels passing on this divine knowledge to the ego, and it is important that the ego pick up on what is being passed on to it, and not turn away.

12
Paragraphs 748-758,
Assumption of Mary and Summary

The chief topic tonight concerns the new dogma of the Assumption of the Virgin Mary. In November of 1950 Pope Pius XII proclaimed as dogma the bodily assumption of the Virgin Mary into heaven. Now this image and idea had been prominent in the Church for almost a thousand years. There has been a feast day of the Assumption of the Virgin, which is held on August 15 of each year. This image of the Assumption and Coronation of the Virgin into heaven is a major image in medieval Christian art, so the image has been around for a long time. What's new is that it has been dogmatized.

Here's what the art historian James Hall says about it:

> For many centuries celebrated as a Church festival, the Assumption was in 1950 declared an article of faith by Pius XII. There is no scriptural foundation for the belief which rests on the apocryphal literature of the 3rd and 4th cents., and on the Tradition of the Catholic Church. It forms the continuation of the narrative of the DEATH OF THE VIRGIN. The 13th cent., a period when the cult of the Virgin was ardently fostered, saw the appearance of the *Golden Legend,* a popular source-book for artists, in which the apocryphal story was retold. [According to this story] As the apostles were sitting by the Virgin's tomb on the third day, [after she had been buried for three days] Christ appeared to them along with St. Michael who brought with him the Virgin's soul. "And anon the soul came again to the body of Mary [which] issued gloriously out of the tomb, and thus was received in the heavenly chamber [with] a great company of angels with her."[107]

A corresponding image is that of the Coronation of the Virgin. In this image the Virgin Mary is shown as already having arrived in heaven, and Christ is in the act of placing a crown on her head.

I want to read you a portion of the proclamation of Pope Pius XII

---

[107] James Hall, *Dictionary of Subjects and Symbols in Art,* p. 34.

to give you the flavor of this. Jung considered the dogma of the Assumption of Mary to be "the most important religious event since the Reformation."[108] It's an astonishing remark. The proclamation of Pope Pius XII is a lengthy document in which the ancient sources are extensively quoted. What I am going to read you is only a small portion of it. The book on Church teachings that I'm quoting from introduces it with this statement:

> On November 1, 1950, Pope Pius XII defined the Assumption of the Blessed Virgin into heaven as a dogma of faith, leaving the dispute about whether or not Mary died an open question. The Pope responded to the petitions of the bishops and the priests and the faithful by giving honor to the Blessed Virgin with this solemn definition. The Assumption of the Blessed Virgin, body and soul, into heaven is another of the great privileges conceded to her by God for consenting to be His mother.[109]

And here is the quote from the proclamation of the dogma:

> The Universal Church in which the Spirit of Truth dwells [remember that I've already spoken of how the Church has taken over the Holy Ghost as its own, and here that's explicitly stated; the Spirit of Truth is a synonym for the Holy Ghost], and which he infallibly guides to perfect knowledge of revealed truths, has shown its faith many times in the course of the centuries. Bishops from all over the world with almost perfect unanimity have petitioned that the truth of the corporeal Assumption of the Blessed Virgin Mary into heaven be defined as dogma of the divine Catholic faith. The truth of this dogma is based on sacred scripture and is deeply rooted in the hearts of the faithful. It is sanctioned by the worship of the Church in the most ancient times. It is completely consonant with all other revealed truths. It has been explained and proclaimed by the study, the knowledge and wisdom of theologians. In consideration of all these reasons, We judge that in God's providence the time has come to proclaim solemnly this wonderful privilege of the Virgin Mary. . . .
> We therefore, after humbly and repeatedly praying to God, and calling upon the light of the Spirit of Truth, the glory of almighty God, who has shown great and particular love for the Virgin Mary,

---

[108] "Answer to Job," *Psychology and Religion,* CW 11, par. 752.
[109] Jesuit Fathers of St. Mary's College (St. Mary's, Kansas), *The Church Teaches: Documents of the Church in English Translation,* p. 212.

for the honor of his Son, the king of immortal ages and the conqueror of sin and death, for the increase of the glory of his great mother, for the joy and exaltation of the whole Church, by the authority of our Lord Jesus Christ, of the blessed apostles Peter and Paul, and by Our own authority, do pronounce, declare and define as a divinely revealed dogma: The Immaculate Mother of God, Mary ever Virgin, after her life on earth, was assumed, body and soul, to the glory of heaven.[110]

That's the proclamation Jung considers the most important religious event since the Reformation. He discusses this matter further in *Mysterium Coniunctionis,* where he points out that the Assumption of Mary into heaven changes the Trinity into a quaternity:

The Christian Trinity is able to maintain itself as such only by eliminating the fourth protagonist of the divine drama. If he were included there would be, not a Trinity, but a Christian Quaternity. For a long time there had been a psychological need for this, as evident from the medieval pictures of the Assumption and Coronation of the Virgin. . . . The recent promulgation of the dogma of the Assumption emphasizes the taking up not only of the soul but of the body of Mary into the Trinity, thus making a dogmatic reality of those medieval representations of the quaternity which are constructed on the following pattern:[111]

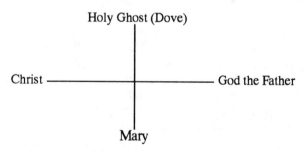

The above pattern is a quaternity embodying the terms Christ, Holy Ghost and God the Father, which is the Trinity, with the fourth added term, Mary.

---

[110] Ibid., p. 213.

[111] *Mysterium Coniunctionis,* CW 14, par. 237; see also Edinger, *The Christian Archetype,* p. 134.

Now it is very interesting how, as with so many of these religious and metaphysical images, alchemy has picked up the image of the Assumption and applied it to the alchemical opus. There are a number of alchemical pictures which depict the Assumption and Coronation of the Virgin Mary as a part of the alchemical procedure. Alchemy functions as an intermediary between the religious context of the imagery and its modern psychological context. Alchemy serves the function of plucking the image out of its religious context and depositing it in the alchemical context—the context of working in the laboratory. And then Jung came along and plucked the images of alchemy out of their alchemical context and placed them squarely into the psyche. But we really need that intermediate operation because it demonstrates that it is the psyche itself which is taking the images out of the religious context, and it demonstrates that the human ego isn't doing it arbitrarily. It has already been done for us by the psyche.

I have placed on the board a remarkable example of such an alchemical picture (next page). It is reproduced from Reusner's *Pandora*. I talk about this picture in *The Christian Archetype* because it is just a marvelous example of how the alchemical process has been superimposed on the metaphysical image.[112]

The picture has an upper level and a lower level. On the upper level Mary has just arrived in heaven and been crowned. God the Father is on one side of her and God the Son is on the other side, with God the Holy Ghost represented as a dove above her. With her arrival in heaven the Trinity has been turned into a quaternity. At the lower level a hunk of amorphous matter is pictured, and a strange, bizarre creature is being pulled out of that lump. Jung describes the picture as the extraction of Mercurius from the *prima materia:*

> The extracted spirit appears in monstrous form . . . the arms are snakes and the lower half of the body resembles a stylized fish's tail. . . . This is without doubt the *anima mundi* who has been freed from the shackles of matter, the *filius macrocosmi* . . . who, because of his double nature, is not only spiritual and physical but unites in himself the morally highest and lowest.[113]

---

112 *The Christian Archetype,* p. 135. See also *Psychology and Alchemy,* CW 12, fig. 232.

113 *Mysterium Coniunctionis,* CW 14, par. 238.

Coronation of the Virgin and the Extraction of Mercurius
(from Reusner's *Pandora*, 1588)

This is an astonishing image to be superimposed upon the celestial phenomenon of Mary being welcomed into heaven—a freakish creature as an embodiment of the spirit Mercurius being pulled out of crude matter.

Here's what Jung says about the Assumption in paragraph 748:

> The nuptial union [between the Trinity and Mary] in the *thalamus* (bridal-chamber) signifies the *hieros gamos*, and this in turn is the first step towards incarnation, towards the birth of the saviour who, since antiquity, was thought of as the *filius solis et lunae*, the *filius sapientiae*, and the equivalent of Christ. When, therefore, a longing for the exaltation of the Mother of God passes through the people, this tendency, if thought to its logical conclusion, means the desire for the birth of a saviour, a peacemaker, a "mediator pacem faciens inter inimicos" [mediator making peace between enemies]. Although he is already born in the pleroma, his birth in time can only be accomplished when it is perceived, recognized, and declared by man.

What Jung is here telling us is that the birth of the savior which follows the *hieros gamos* corresponds to the extraction of Mercurius from the lump of the *prima materia*. That's the savior birth as it appears alchemically.

Then again, in paragraph 755:

> The dogmatization of the *Assumptio Mariae* points to the *hieros gamos* in the pleroma, and this in turn implies, as we have said, the future birth of the divine child who, in accordance with the divine trend towards incarnation, will choose as his birthplace the empirical man.

So that amorphous lump from which Mercurius is being extracted is the empirical man, the empirical you and I, empirical man and woman. Jung continues in paragraph 755:

> The metaphysical process is known to the psychology of the unconscious as the individuation process.

The reason Jung can grant such superlative importance to the dogma of the Assumption is because he recognizes that promulgation of the dogma of the Assumption occurs synchronistically—simultaneously with his discovery and elaboration of the *coniunctio*—because it happens that that dogma was proclaimed in 1950 in the middle of the same decade in which Jung spelled out the psychology of the *coniunctio* in his two works, *Psychology of the Transference,* first published in 1946, and *Mysterium Coniunctionis,* first published in 1955. The dogma of the Assumption synchronistically coincides with the discovery of the *coniunctio.*

This announcement of the Assumption of Mary bodily into heaven is the latest event in the process of the transformation of the God-image. The God-image has now been transformed from a Trinity into a quaternity. With the addition of the feminine and corporeal aspects of existence, together with all the dark qualities that belong to flesh, the God-image now has been completed so that it contains the complete range of opposites—male/female, spirit/earth, good/evil.

Summary

With our remaining time I'd like to review the book we've been through, to remind you of its basic content. In the first sentence of *Answer to Job* you remember that Jung speaks of the long historical development or evolutionary process of the divine drama. I emphasized that phrase, "divine drama." This sentence strikes the keynote for the entire book, because *Answer to Job* lays before us a grand panorama of the evolution of the God-image as it has taken place in the Western psyche. Let me remind you of what the stages have been.

We first take up the God-image in the polymorphous confusion of early Greek pantheism which gradually unified loosely under the hegemony of Zeus. The other deities, however, were permitted considerable autonomy, so that perpetual conflicts and arguments took place in the divine realm. In addition, Zeus was not particularly interested in human beings. He had no need for them. Nevertheless human beings were forced to endure the conflicts of the gods, who were perpetually interfering with human affairs on earth. They had to put up with being victimized by these warring gods without the compensation of redemptive meaning to explain what was going on. That means then that life in antiquity was essentially tragic, just by its nature.

But the God-image underwent a radical transformation with the arrival of Yahweh as the tribal god of a small band of Semitic herdsmen. Yahweh needed man in order to realize himself, and he therefore made a contract with Israel to be their one God, and thus monotheism was born. Very shortly afterward Yahweh revealed that he was not just a tribal god, but the universal Creator God whose scope included the whole universe. Yahweh was a mixture of opposites: he was both loving and wrathful, creative and destructive. At times he was profoundly kind and merciful, and other times he would fall into tantrums of destructive rage. And always he demanded praise and glory for himself, and he required constant bloody animal sacrifices to propitiate him.

The next major transformation occurred following Job's encounter with Yahweh. By holding to his integrity, his consciousness, Job was granted a glimpse of Yahweh's backside—the abysmal world of shards; and he came to realize that Yahweh was a phenomenon and not a man. At this point human ego consciousness surpassed God's consciousness, and in order to catch up Yahweh was obliged to rectify his crime against man by becoming man himself, by incarnating. And so Christ the son of Yahweh was born—the good son. His life performed a double function:

1) He preached a new image of God, namely that of a loving father in whom there is no darkness.

2) As the incarnated Yahweh who had wronged Job, he submitted himself to punishment for that crime, and as Jung tells us:

> As a consequence the sacrifice was a self-destruction of the amoral God, incarnated in a mortal body. Thus the sacrifice takes on the aspect of a highly moral deed, of a self-punishment, as it were.[114]

At the same time that Christ the good son of Yahweh was born, however, Satan the evil son was cast out of heaven, so that a decisive *separatio* took place in the God-image, with the dark evil aspect being split off and repressed. However, the Book of Revelation predicts that at the end of the aeon there will be a return of the repressed through *enantiodromia* and we will then be dealing with the opposite of the good son.

Then in the early Christian centuries the doctrine of God as the Trinity was elaborated. Femininity was not visible, though traces of

---

[114] *Letters,* vol. 2, p. 313; see also above, p. 95.

it may be found in the androgyny of Christ and also in the connections that the Holy Ghost retains symbolically with Aphrodite. Notably they share the image of the dove.

Finally in the Christian aeon, in accordance with the *enantiodromia* I just referred to, the God-image undergoes another massive transformation which is indicated by the image of the Assumption of Mary into heaven. Now the Trinitarian god has become a quaternity, and fleshly humanity, with all of its darkness and ambiguity, has become part of the totality. This indicates a second *hieros gamos* in the pleroma, to be followed by a further incarnation, this time in sinful man, which will bring about the "Christification of many" [par. 758], which Jung says is known psychologically as individuation.

*

In the last few minutes I would like to give the final words to Jung. I've culled out a few quotations, sequentially, to remind you of the content of *Answer to Job*.

> I grieve for you my brother. [Epigraph, modified]

> In what follows I shall speak of the venerable objects of religious belief. Whoever talks of such matters inevitably runs the risk of being torn to pieces by the two parties who are in mortal conflict about those very things. [par. 553]

> "Physical" is not the only criterion of truth: there are also *psychic truths*. [par. 553]

> The statements made in the Holy Scriptures are also utterances of the soul. [par. 557]

> The Book of Job serves as a paradigm for a certain experience of God which has a very special significance for our time. [par. 562, modified]

> Existence is only real when it is conscious to somebody. That is why the Creator needs conscious man. [par. 575]

> Because of his littleness, puniness, and defenselessness against the Almighty [man] possesses . . . a somewhat keener consciousness based on self-reflection. [par. 579]

Job is no more than the outward occasion for an inward process of dialectic in God. [par. 587]

Job is challenged as though he himself were a god. [par. 594]

Mortal man is raised by his moral behaviour above the stars in heaven, from which position of advantage he can behold the back of Yahweh, the abysmal world of "shards." [par. 595]

The naive assumption that the creator of the world is a conscious being must be regarded as a disastrous prejudice. [par. 600, n. 13]

Whoever knows God has an effect on him. The failure of the attempt to corrupt Job has changed Yahweh's nature. [par. 617]

Yahweh had lost sight of his pleromatic coexistence with Sophia. [par. 620]

Wisdom reveals herself to men as a friendly helper and advocate. [par. 623]

God desires to regenerate himself in the mystery of the heavenly nuptials. [par. 624]

[When God becomes man] it means nothing less than a world-shaking transformation of God. [par. 631]

God is Reality itself and therefore—last but not least—man. This realization is a millennial process. [par. 631]

Yahweh must become man precisely because he has done man a wrong. [par. 640]

As a result of the partial neutralization of Satan, Yahweh identifies with his light aspect and becomes the good God. [par. 651]

The attempt to secure an absolute and final victory for good is bound to lead to a dangerous accumulation of evil and hence to catastrophe. [par. 653]

The continuing, direct operation of the Holy Ghost on those who are called to be God's children implies . . . a broadening process of incarnation. [par. 658]

All opposites are of God, therefore man must bend to this burden; and in so doing he finds that God in his "oppositeness" has taken possession of him, incarnated himself in him. He becomes a vessel filled with divine conflict. [par. 659]

The *imago Dei* pervades the whole human sphere and is involuntarily represented by mankind. [par. 660, modified]

[Ezekiel's] first great vision is made up of two well-ordered compound quaternities . . . [and their quintessence] is represented by a figure which has "the likeness of a human form." [par. 665]

Ezekiel grasped, in a symbol, the fact that Yahweh was drawing closer to man. [par. 667]

The encounter with the creature changes the creator. . . . The two main climaxes are formed firstly by the Job tragedy, and secondly by Ezekiel's revelation. [par. 686]

[The Paraclete, or Holy Ghost (the Spirit of Truth and Wisdom)] from now on shall make his abode in creaturely man. Since he is the Third Person of the Deity, this is as much as to say that *God will be begotten in creaturely man.* [par. 692]

The future indwelling of the Holy Ghost in man amounts to a continuing incarnation of God. [par. 693]

[In the sun-moon woman episode in Revelation] the man-child is "caught up" to God. . . . This would seem to indicate that the child-figure will remain latent for an indefinite time and that its activity is reserved for the future. [The future is now.] [par. 713]

John's problem was not a personal one. . . . What burst upon him is the storm of the times, premonition of a tremendous enantiodromia. [par. 717]

God has a terrible double aspect: a sea of grace is met by a seething lake of fire, and the light of love glows with a fierce dark heat . . . it burns but gives no light. That is the eternal, as distinct from the temporal, gospel: *one can love God but must fear him.* [par. 733]

God acts out of the unconscious of man and forces him to harmonize and unite the opposing influences to which his mind is exposed from the unconscious. The unconscious wants both: to divide and to unite. . . . God wants to become man, but not quite. [par. 740]

Everything now depends on man. [par. 745]

Since the apocalypse we now know again that God is not only to be loved but also to be feared. He fills us with evil as well as with good, otherwise he would not need to be feared; and because he wants to become man, the uniting of his antinomy must take place in man. . . . [Man] can no longer remain blind and unconscious. He must know something of God's nature and of metaphysical processes if he is to understand himself and thereby achieve gnosis of the Divine. [par. 747]

The dogma of the Assumption [of the Virgin Mary] . . . I consider to be the most important religious event since the Reformation. [par. 752]

The dogmatization of the *Assumptio Mariae* points to the *hieros gamos* in the pleroma, and this in turn implies . . . the future birth of the divine child, who, in accordance with the divine trend towards incarnation, will choose as his birthplace the empirical man. The metaphysical process is known to the psychology of the unconscious as the individuation process. [par. 755]

The indwelling of the Holy Ghost, the third Divine Person, in man, brings about a Christification of many. . . . [In order to avoid inflation in such a situation one must remember the thorn in the flesh of St. Paul.] That is to say, even the enlightened person remains what he is, and is never more than his own limited ego before the One who dwells within him, whose form has no knowable boundaries, who encompasses him on all sides, fathomless as the abysms of the earth and vast as the sky. [par. 758]

And with that remark Jung ends *Answer to Job* and I end this course.

Bibliography

Adler, Gerhard, "Aspects of Jung's Psychology." *Psychological Perspectives,* vol. 6, no. 1 (Spring 1975).

F.H. Borsch, *The Son of Man in Myth and History.* Philadelphia: Westminster Press, 1967.

Charles, R.H., ed. *The Apocrypha and the Pseudepigrapha of the Old Testament in English.* 2 vols. London: Oxford University Press, 1969.

Edinger, Edward F. *An American Jungian: Edward F. Edinger in Conversation with Lawrence Jaffe.* Videotape. Produced and directed by Dianne Cordic, Los Angeles.

_____. *Anatomy of the Psyche: Alchemical Symbolism in Psychotherapy.* La Salle, IL: Open Court Publishing Company, 1985.

_____. *The Bible and the Psyche: Individuation Symbolism in the Old Testament.* Toronto: Inner City Books, 1986.

_____. *The Christian Archetype: A Jungian Commentary on the Life of Christ.* Toronto: Inner City Books, 1987.

_____. *The Creation of Consciousness: Jung's Myth for Modern Man.* Toronto: Inner City Books, 1984.

_____. *Ego and Archetype: Individuation and the Religious Function of the Psyche.* New York: Putnam, 1972.

_____. *Encounter with the Self: A Jungian Commentary on William Blake's* Illustrations of the Book of Job. Toronto: Inner City Books, 1986.

_____. *Goethe's* Faust: *Notes for a Jungian Commentary.* Toronto: Inner City Books, 1990.

_____. *The Living Psyche: A Jungian Analysis in Pictures.* Wilmette, IL: Chiron Publications, 1990.

_____. *Melville's Moby-Dick: A Jungian Commentary.* New York: New Directions, 1978.

Emerson, Ralph Waldo. *Essays.* New York: Houghton Mifflin Co., 1883.

Hall, James. *Dictionary of Subjects and Symbols in Art.* New York: Harper and Row (Icon Editions), 1979.

Harding, M. Esther. *The Parental Image.* New York: G.P. Putnam's Sons, 1965.

136

Jaffe, Lawrence W. *Liberating the Heart: Spirituality and Jungian Psychology.* Toronto: Inner City Books, 1990.

Jesuit Fathers of St. Mary's College. *The Church Teaches: Documents of the Church in English Translation.* Rockford, IL: Tan Books, 1973.

Jung, C.G. *The Collected Works* (Bollingen Series XX). 20 vols. Trans. R.F.C. Hull. Ed. H. Read, M. Fordham, G. Adler, Wm. McGuire. Princeton: Princeton University Press, 1953-1979.

_____. *Letters* (Bollingen Series XCV). 2 vols. Trans. R.F.C. Hull. Ed. Gerhard Adler, Aniela Jaffé. Princeton: Princeton University Press, 1973.

_____. *Memories, Dreams, Reflections.* Ed. Aniela Jaffé. New York: Pantheon Books, 1961.

_____. *Nietzsche's* Zarathustra: *Notes of the Seminar Given in 1934-1939* (Bollingen Series XCIX). 2 vols. Ed. James L. Jarrett. Princeton: Princeton University Press, 1988.

_____. *The Visions Seminars.* 2 vols. Zürich: Spring Publications, 1976.

Kluger, Rivkah Scharf. *Satan in the Old Testament.* Trans. Hildegard Nagel. Evanston, IL: Northwestern University Press, 1967.

_____. *Psyche and Bible.* New York: Spring Publications and the Analytical Psychology Club of New York, 1974..

Kurth, W., ed. *The Complete Woodcuts of Albrecht Dürer.* New York: Dover, 1963.

Lem, Stanislav. *A Perfect Vacuum.* New York: Harcourt Brace Jovanovich, 1983.

Milton, John. *Milton: Complete Poetry and Selected Prose.* Ed. E.H. Visiak. Glasgow: The Nonesuch Library, University Press, 1969.

von Franz, Marie-Louise. *Aurora Consurgens.* Trans. R.F.C. Hull and A.S.B. Glover. New York: Pantheon Books, 1966.

_____. *C.G. Jung: His Myth in Our Time.* Trans. William H. Kennedy. New York: G.P. Putnam's Sons, 1975.

Index

Abel, 61, 65
active imagination, 34, 77
Adam, 61, 65
affect, 35-37
Aion, 11, 18, 21-22, 65, 83
alchemy, 21-22, 56, 71-72, 81, 90,
    114, 117, 127
amplification, 107-110
analysis, practice of, 31, 36, 61, 65-
    67, 77, 80, 93, 98-99, 119-120
Anatomy of the Psyche, The, 74,
    104, 109
Ancient of Days, 84
angels, 74-75, 85-86, 106, 113,
    122-123
anima, 30, 57, 60, 62
anima mundi, 127
animal sacrifice, 94, 131
animism, 32-33
animus, 57, 60
Answer to Job: genesis of, 11, 17-
    19, 21-22, 65
    importance to Jung, 20-21
    meaning of title, 19
Anthropos, 90
Antichrist, 11-12, 21-22
antinomy, 37, 40, 49, 121
anxiety, 113-114, 121
Aphrodite, 132
Apocalypse, 132
apocalyptic imagery, 100-103
Apocrypha, 54-55
archetypes/archetypal imag(es),
    28-31, 53, 56, 62, 66, 68-69,
    77, 81, 87, 89-90, 95, 98
    100, 106-110, 115, 120

archetypus mundus, 56
Assumption of Virgin Mary,
    124-130, 132
atheism, 92-93
Augustine, 116
Aurora Consurgens, 56
auseinandersetzung, 89
autism, 43
Axiom of Maria, 85

Babylon, 100, 114-117
Behemoth, 86
Blake, William, 36
book of life, 117-118

Cabala, 50-51
Cain, 61
cancer phobia, 13-14
Cantilena, 117
catastrophe, reaction to, 40-41
cathedra, 107
chair archetype, 107
child: divine, 127
    spoiled, 45
Chochma, 53
chosen people, 43-44, 60
Christ, 11-12, 56, 61, 63, 66-67, 70,
    72-78, 83, 89, 91, 93-98, 104-
    105, 117, 124-126, 131-132
Christian Archetype, The, 127
Christianity, 11-12, 21-22, 72, 74-
    78, 80, 83, 97-98, 116-118,
    121, 124, 130-132
"Christification of many," 132
*Chymical Wedding of Christian
    Rosencreutz,* 109

city archetype, 115-116
coagulatio, 74, 109-110
collective unconscious, 12-14, 28, 35-37, 53, 64, 68, 71-72, 80-82, 100, 120
compensation, 47-48, 63, 66-67, 98-99, 115
completeness, 66-67, 111
complex(es), 13-14, 52, 60
complexio oppositorum, 22, 119
conflict, 25, 70-71, 80-81, 121, 130
coniunctio, 49, 109, 112, 119, 129-130
consciousness:
    birth of, 32-33, 58
    and conflict, 70-71
    of contrasexual other, 57
    development of, 45-50, 58, 61
    effect on God, 61-64, 73
    and God-image, 11-12, 19
    transpersonal dimension, 52
container, and contained, 58-59
continuing incarnation, 77-78, 96-97, 112
Coronation of the Virgin, 124, 127-128
covenant, 39-40, 60, 131
Creation of Consciousness, The, 42
creationists, 33
creativity, 69-70
creature, and creator, 92-93
credo containment, 92-93
crucifixion, 70, 91

damned souls, 118
Daniel's vision, 82, 84, 89, 106
David, and Jonathan, 24-26
differentiation, 82-85, 88-89
Dionysos, 70
discrimination, 104-106

dismemberment, 70
divine child, 127
divine drama, 32-34, 49, 57, 69, 91, 130
dream(s): 13, 32, 53, 73, 98-99, 107
    of ape-like man, 42-43
    archetypal, 123
    of being marked, 109
    of book of life, 117
    collective imagery in, 120-121
    compensatory, 98-99
    of end of the world, 100-103
    of giants, 87
    of pie divided up, 111
    of piece of moon falling, 109
    reconciling symbols in, 121
    of terrorists, 110
    threatening, 119
Dürer, Albrecht, 104-105

Ecclesiasticus, 54-55
ego: and archetype, 68-69
    contained by creed, 92
    first- and second-stage, 25
    as incarnating agent, 74-75, 89
    relativization of, 100-101
    and Self, 28-30, 43-51, 57-60, 62, 69, 76-77, 89, 92-93, 100-101, 116, 118
    and shadow, 30-31
    and suffering, 36-37
    transformation of, 36-37, 89
Ego and Archetype, 45, 110
Eighty-ninth Psalm, 39
elixir permanens, 81
Emerson, Ralph Waldo, 47-48
En Soph, 50
enantiodromia, 11, 66, 120, 131-132
end of the world archetype, 100-103
Enoch, Book of, 74, 82, 84-87, 89

Eros, 63-64
evil, 21-22, 30-31, 37, 51, 73-74,
    121, 130
evolution, 32-33, 93
Exodus, 38-39
Eye of God, 100
Ezekiel's vision, 82-85, 89, 91, 98,
    118-119

fallen angels, 74-75, 85-86, 122-123
Faust, 88
feminine principle, 66-67, 130-132
filius macrocosmi, 127
filius philosophorum, 90
fire, lake of, 100, 113-114, 117
First Man, 50
flood, 87
Freud, Sigmund, 30

Genesis, 33, 74
giants, 86-87
Gnosticism, 53, 55-56, 68, 74
God *(see also* God-image *and*
    Yahweh):
    as autonomous power, 14
    becoming man, 71-72, 88-89
    need for man, 78
    as neurosis, 13
    objectivation of, 71
    as reality, 19, 71
    unconsciousness of, 12, 19, 34,
    42
God-image *(see also* God, Yahweh
    and passim):
    anthropomorphic, 16, 21, 24
    as ape-like, 43
    bipolar nature, 11
    compensation in, 47
    conflict in, 81, 121-122
    Daniel's vision, 84-85

differentiation of, 82-85, 88-89
evolution of, 130-132
Ezekiel's vision, 82-85
imago Dei, 80-81
Jung's experience of, 12-19, 51
opposites in, 121-122
three Western versions of, 11-12
transformation of, 12, 36-39, 41,
    82-91, 130-132
unified, in Jungian aeon, 112
Yahwistic, 17, 73
Goethe, 88
grace, sea of, 113-114

Hall, James, 124
Harding, M. Esther, 17, 107
heavenly Jerusalem, 100, 115-116,
    118-119
Hebrews, Book of, 94-95
Helen of Troy, 55-56
heresy, 97
hermaphrodite archetype, 119
hieros gamos, 54, 64-65, 119, 129,
    132
Holy Ghost/Spirit, 96-97, 126-128,
    132
homunculus, 71

identification, 35, 38, 43, 57-58, 70,
    76, 87, 121
Iliad, 38-39, 56
Illustrations of the Book of Job, 36
imago Dei, 80-81
incarnation: 12, 19, 65-66, 69, 71
    74-78, 80, 88-90, 96-97, 112,
    129, 131
    continuing, 77-78, 96-97, 112
individuation, 44, 78, 92-93, 109,
    129, 132
infidelity complex, 59-60

inflation, 23, 45, 69-70, 76, 87, 92
injustice, 47
Israel, 44, 57, 59-60, 62-63, 106
   131

Jacob, 29
Jaffé, Aniela, 17
Jeremiah, 59
Jerusalem, 100, 115-116, 118-119
Jews, 43-44, 116
Job: archetype, 19, 28-31
   Book of, 28-30, 32-36, 63
   encounter with Yahweh, 12, 28-
      30, 32-37, 40-41, 44-45, 47,
      49-52, 70-71, 82-83, 95, 131
   as neurotic, 30
John, Book of, 76-77, 98
John, St. *(see also* Revelation,
   Book of), 18-19, 113
Jonathan, and David, 24-26
Jung, C.G.: experience of God-
   image, 12-19, 51
   experience of *hieros gamos,* 64-65
   letter to Aniela Jaffé, 17
   letter to Elined Kotschnig, 33-34,
      78, 95
   letter to Erich Neumann, 15
   letter to Father Lachat, 96-97
   letter to Victor White, 29-30
justice, 47-48

Kluger, Rivkah, 44, 52
Kotschnig, Elined, 33-34, 78, 95

Lachat, Father, 96
lake of fire, 100, 113-114, 117
lamb, sacrificial, 93-95
Last Judgment, 86, 90, 100, 110,
   117
Lectori Benevolo, 23-28

Lem, Stanislav, 79
life cycle, psychic, 45-47
Logion of Jesus, 97-98
Logos, 56, 104
Lord's Prayer, 75-76

mandalas, 83, 100, 115
marked ones, 108-109
marriage, 57-60, 63-64
"Marriage As a Psychological
   Relationship," 57-59
Marriage of the Lamb, 64, 100,
   118-119
masculine principle, 66-67
matter, 55, 73-74, 129-130
Matthew, Book of, 75
Memories, Dreams, Reflections,
   18, 64, 119
Mephistopheles, 88
Mercurius, 127-129
Milton, John, 74-75
Monoïmos, 27
monotheism, 38-39
Mysterium Coniunctionis, 22, 65,
   126, 130
mystic marriage, *see hieros gamos*
mysticism, Jewish, 83

narcissism, 42-43
Neumann, Erich, 15
neurosis, 13-14, 30
Nietzsche, Friedrich, 69-70
Noah, 87
"Non Serviam," 79-80
numinosity, 49-50
numinosum, 103-104, 112

objective psyche, *see* collective
   unconscious
one third, 110-111

opposites: 11-12, 16, 18, 21-23, 37, 66-67, 73-74, 80-81, 89, 109, 120-122, 131
reconciliation of, 121

Pandora, 127-128
Paraclete, 76-78, 96-97
"Paradise Lost," 74-75
patterns, pre-existing, 65-66, 68
Pentecost, 97
perfection, 63, 66-67, 120
petitions, in Lord's Prayer, 75-76
Philosophers' Stone, 71-72, 90
pleroma, 55, 60, 67-68, 88, 91-92, 113, 129, 132
polytheism, 38-39
power, 16, 38, 63-64, 78
prima materia, 56, 71, 127, 129
privatio boni, 21
projection, 57, 59-60, 62
Proverbs, 53-54
psyche, reality of, 26-28, 33
Psyche and Bible, 44
psychic life cycle, 45-47
Psychology of the Transference, The, 65, 130
psychosis, 101
puer aeternus, 111

reality of the psyche, 26-28, 33
reconciling symbols, 121
redemption, 22, 38, 52, 56, 90, 130
reductionism, 26, 29-30, 90
relationship, 57-59, 63-64
repressed, return of, 117, 131
resurrection, 117
Reusner, 127-128
Revelation, Book of, 18, 73, 94, 99-120, 131
revelations, 98

Ripley, 117

sacrifice, 93-98, 131
salvator macrocosmi, 71-72
Sapientia Dei, 53, 56
sarcasm, 15-16
Satan, 12, 22, 28, 40, 61, 73-75, 86-88, 100, 109, 131
Satan in the Old Testament, 52
Saul, King, 24-26
scapegoat, 59
science-fiction, 79-80
sea of grace, 113-114
sefirotic tree, 50, 64
Self: city as aspect of, 115
and ego, 28-30, 43-51, 57-60, 62, 69, 76-77, 89, 92-93, 100-101, 116, 118
identification with, 38, 43-44, 76
as instrument of discrimination, 104-106
Jung's formula, 83
as menacing, 119
as Son of Man, 90-91
separatio, 51, 73-74, 83, 104, 112, 131
seven, 99, 103-104, 106-108
shadow, 30-31
shards, 50-51, 61, 131
Shiva, 70
Shulamite, 54, 56
Simon Magus, 55
Sol-Luna *coniunctio,* 112
Solomon's Seal, 114
Son of Man, 84, 86, 89-91, 99, 107
Song of Songs, 54
Sophia, 53-57, 60, 62-64, 74, 115, 119
soul, 27-28
souls, damned, 118

Star of David, 114
stars, 108-109
suffering, 19, 36, 47, 52, 78, 90
sun, as sawblade, 104
sun-moon woman, 99, 111-112, 115
sword, 99, 104, 112
symbols, 90, 121
synchronicity, 68

tertium non datur, 121
Tertullian, 27
third, 110-111
three *(see also* Trinity), 111
throne vision, 99, 106-107
transference, 77
transformation, 12, 36-39, 45-50,
    63-64, 71-72, 130-132
"Transformation Symbolism in the
    Mass," 95
Trinity, 96, 110-111, 126-127,
    130-132
Trojan War, 38
two wives archetype, 62

unconscious: activation of, 87, 100,
    102-103
  compensatory function, 47-48
  experience of, 12-19
  humanization of, 71-72, 88-89
  need to be seen, 42-43, 89-91,
    122
  as Yahweh, 35-37, 51
unconsciousness, 12, 19, 34, 42, 51

vessels, breaking of, 50-51
Virgin Mary, 12, 124-130
visions: 82-85, 89, 91, 98-101, 104,
    106-107, 111-112, 118-120

Daniel's, 82, 84, 89, 106
Ezekiel's, 82-85
Visions Seminars, 12
von Franz, Marie-Louise, 20, 56

water, 114
White, Victor, 29-30
Whore of Babylon, 100, 114-117
Wisdom *(see also* Sophia), 53-56, 63
Wisdom of Solomon, 55

Yahweh *(see also* God *and* God-
    image): as affect, 35
  as antinomy, 37, 40, 121
  conflict in, 50
  covenant with, 39-40, 60, 131
  and creativity, 69-70
  and Israel, 44, 57, 59-60, 62-63,
    106, 131
  and Job, 11-12, 28-30, 40-41,
    44-45, 70 *and passim*
  as mixture of opposites, 131
  morality of, 16, 51, 89, 95, 131
  as phenomenon, 51, 71, 131
  and sacrifice, 95
  as Son of Man, 90
  and Sophia, 53-54, 57, 119
  tamed by Virgin, 12
  transformation of, 12, 38, 41, 47,
    63-64, 71-72, 122, 130-132
  as the unconscious, 35-37, 51, 53
  unconsciousness of, 12, 19, 34,
    42, 51
  and Zeus, 38

Zarathustra, 69-70
Zeus, 38, 64, 130
Zion, 116

Studies in Jungian Psychology
by Jungian Analysts

Sewn Paperbacks

Addiction to Perfection: The Still Unravished Bride
Marion Woodman (Toronto). ISBN 0-919123-11-2. Illustrated. 208 pp. $17pb/$22hc

Alchemy: An Introduction to the Symbolism and the Psychology.
Marie-Louise von Franz (Zurich). ISBN 0-919123-04-X. 84 illustrations. 288 pp. $18

Descent to the Goddess: A Way of Initiation for Women
Sylvia Brinton Perera (New York). ISBN 0-919123-05-8. 112 pp. $14

The Creation of Consciousness: Jung's Myth for Modern Man
Edward F. Edinger, M.D. (Los Angeles). ISBN 0-919123-13-9. Illustrated. 128 pp. $14

The Illness That We Are: A Jungian Critique of Christianity
John P. Dourley (Ottawa). ISBN 0-919123-16-3. 128 pp. $14

The Pregnant Virgin: A Process of Psychological Transformation
Marion Woodman (Toronto). ISBN 0-919123-20-1. Illustrated. 208 pp. $17pb/$22hc

The Jungian Experience: Analysis and Individuation
James A. Hall, M.D. (Dallas). ISBN 0-919123-25-2. 176 pp. $16

The Christian Archetype: A Jungian Commentary on the Life of Christ
Edward F. Edinger, M.D. (Los Angeles). ISBN 0-919123-27-9. Illustrated. 144 pp. $15

Personality Types: Jung's Model of Typology
Daryl Sharp (Toronto). ISBN 0-919123-30-9. Diagrams. 128 pp. $14

The Sacred Prostitute: Eternal Aspect of the Feminine
Nancy Qualls-Corbett (Birmingham). ISBN 0-919123-31-7. Illustrated. 176 pp. $16

The Survival Papers: Anatomy of a Midlife Crisis
Daryl Sharp (Toronto). ISBN 0-919123-34-1. 160 pp. $15

The Cassandra Complex: Living with Disbelief
Laurie Layton Schapira (New York). ISBN 0-919123-35-X. Illustrated. 160 pp. $15

The Ravaged Bridegroom: Masculinity in Women
Marion Woodman (Toronto). ISBN 0-919123-42-2. Illustrated. 224 pp. $18

Liberating the Heart: Spirituality and Jungian Psychology
Lawrence W. Jaffe (Los Angeles). ISBN 0-919123-43-0. 176 pp. $16

The Rainbow Serpent: Bridge to Consciousness
Robert L. Gardner (Toronto). ISBN 0-919123-46-5. Illustrated. 128 pp. $15

Phallos: Sacred Image of the Masculine.
Eugene Monick (Scranton/New York). ISBN 0-919123-26-0. 30 illustrations. 144 pp. $15

The Phallic Quest: Priapus and Masculine Inflation
James Wyly (Chicago). ISBN 0-919123-37-6. 128 pp. $14

Castration and Male Rage: The Phallic Wound
Eugene Monick (Scranton/New York). ISBN 0-919123-51-1. Illustrated. 144 pp. $16

Circle of Care: Clinical Issues in Jungian Psychology
Warren Steinberg (New York). ISBN 0-919123-47-3. 160 pp. $16

Jung Lexicon: A Primer of Terms & Concepts
Daryl Sharp (Toronto). ISBN 0-919123-48-1. Diagrams. 160 pp. $16

Prices and payment (check or money order) in $U.S. (in Canada, $Cdn)
Add Postage/Handling: 1-2 books, $2; 3-4 books, $4; 5-8 books, $7

Complete Catalogue and 36-page SAMPLER free on request

INNER CITY BOOKS
Box 1271, Station Q, Toronto, Canada M4T 2P4